JEWS AND CHRISTIANS

JEWS and CHRISTIANS

Preparation for Dialogue

Edited by
GEORGE A. F. KNIGHT

The Westminster Press
PHILADELPHIA

LIBRARY OF CONGRESS CATALOG CARD NO. 65–11614

PUBLISHED BY THE WESTMINSTER PRESS®

PHILADELPHIA, PENNSYLVANIA

PRINTED IN THE UNITED STATES OF AMERICA

CONTENTS

CONTRIBUTORS

Roswell P. Barnes, who contributed the Foreword, is executive secretary in America for the World Council of Churches and consultant member of the committee on the Church and the Jewish People, of the National Council of Churches' Central Department of Evangelism.

James R. Brown, who contributed Chapter 8, "The One Israel of God," is associate professor of Old Testament at Nashotah House, Nashotah, Wisconsin. He was educated at Oxford University and Kelham College, England, and served in the parochial ministry in England and Canada.

C. J. de Catanzaro, who contributed Chapter 3, "The Meaning of Prophecy," is Lydia Hibbard Professor of Old Testament Literature and Languages, Seabury-Western Theological Seminary, Evanston, Illinois. He received degrees from the University of King's College and Dalhousie University, Halifax, Canada; and Trinity College and the University of Toronto, Toronto, Canada; and Keble College, Oxford, England.

Robert Beach Cunningham, who contributed the Introduction, is acting chairman of the Division of Evangelism of the Board of National Missions of The United Presbyterian Church in the U.S.A., and chairman of the committee on the Church and the Jewish People, of the Central Department of Evangelism, National Council of the Churches of Christ in the U.S.A.

A. Roy Eckardt, who contributed Chapter 9, "Anti-Semitism," is professor of religion at Lehigh University, Bethlehem, Pennsylvania. He received degrees from Yale Divinity School and Union Theological Seminary. A Lilly Endowment scholar in England and Europe, 1963–1964 studying contemporary Jewish-Christian relations, he is the author of *Christianity and the Children of Israel.*

Harold Floreen, who contributed Chapter 6, "The 'Advantage' of the Christian," is professor of ethics and English Bible, Lutheran College and Seminary, Saskatoon, Saskatchewan, Canada. He was educated at Augustana College and Seminary, Rock Island, Illinois; Chicago Lutheran Theological Seminary; and Union Theological Seminary, New York. He served as the executive of the Department for the Christian Approach to the Jewish People of the National Lutheran Council of Churches and was associate director of the corresponding committee under the former International Missionary Council.

Norman K. Gottwald, who contributed Chapter 4, "The Messianic Hope," is Lowry Professor of Old Testament at Andover Newton Theological School, Newton Center, Massachusetts. He was the recipient of a Fulbright Research Scholarship for study at the Hebrew University, Jerusalem, 1960–1961, and is author of *Studies in the Book of Lamentations, A Light to the Nations,* and *All the Kingdoms of the Earth: Israelite Prophecy and International Relations in the Ancient Near East.*

Jakob Jocz, who contributed Chapter 5, "The 'Advantage' of the Jew," is professor of systematic theology at Wycliffe College, Toronto. Clerk in Holy Orders, he studied in Germany, England, and Scotland, and is author of *The Jewish People and Jesus Christ, A Theology of Election,* and *The Spiritual History of Israel.*

George A. F. Knight, who contributed Chapter 2, "The 'Mystery' of Israel," and Chapter 10, "Beyond Dialogue," and who contributed material for Chapter 7, "Building Theological Bridges," is professor of Old Testament, McCormick Theological Seminary, Chicago, Illinois. He received degrees from Glasgow University and Trinity College, Glasgow, and was formerly director of the Scottish School, Budapest, and organized "Jews and Christians House," Glasgow, 1942. He is the author of *From Moses to Paul: A Christological Study in the Light of Our Hebraic Heritage; A Christian Theology of the Old Testament;* and *Law and Grace.*

Frederick Neumann, who contributed material for Chapter 7, "Building Theological Bridges," is a Congregational minister in Brooklyn, New York, and visiting lecturer in Old Testament, The Hartford Seminary Foundation Connecticut. He was educated at the Universities of Freiburg i.B., Germany, and Vienna, Austria; and at the Institutum Judaicum Delitzschianum, Vienna.

Edmund F. Perry, who contributed Chapter 1, "The Peculiar Sociological Situation of the Jews in North America," is professor of the history of religion at Northwestern University, Evanston, Illinois. He received degrees from Emory and Northwestern Universities and is author of *The Gospel in Dispute*.

Ovid R. Sellers, who contributed material for Chapter 1, "The Peculiar Sociological Situation of the Jews in North America," is professor emeritus of Old Testament, McCormick Theological Seminary, Chicago, Illinois. He received degrees from the University of Chicago, McCormick Theological Seminary, and Johns Hopkins University, and was director of the American School of Oriental Research, Jerusalem, in 1948–1949.

FOREWORD

Our generation has been shocked by unprecedented and unspeakably tragic outrages against the Jews in Germany and in other countries of Europe. Elsewhere there has been inexcusable and humiliating discrimination against them. Anti-Semitism has absorbed so much of the attention of Christians when they thought about relations with Jews that consideration of the relations between Jews and Christians as religious groups has been neglected.

The World Council of Churches has vehemently and repeatedly condemned anti-Semitism and has intervened frequently on behalf of Jews under persecution. The Council has considered it advisable at the same time to point out the desirability of giving attention also to relations between Jews and Christians as religious communities in terms of what they hold in common as well as of their theological differences. There has been much confusion at those points among Christians and no clear understanding of the attitudes which they should have toward Jews in terms of religious faith.

Consequently, the World Council has encouraged a Biblical and theological study of the relations between the two faiths so that there may be a better understanding of the differences and the distinctions to be assumed in relationships.

For the initiation of the study in this country, the World Council turned to the Central Department of Evangelism of the National Council of the Churches of Christ in the U.S.A.

to administer the study here. This volume is the first tangible result of the work of scholars solicited by the Department of Evangelism. Although no World Council body has seen the manuscripts or even evaluated the outline of the book, I am confident that this first contribution to the study in this country will be welcomed as the beginning of a Biblical and theological analysis that should help to clarify the thinking of many Christians.

Through the channels of the World Council, this study will be brought into association with studies in Europe and elsewhere. Thus, the ecumenical discourse, which it is hoped will also involve Jewish Scriptural and theological scholars, may lead to a better mutual understanding.

ROSWELL P. BARNES

INTRODUCTION

by

ROBERT BEACH CUNNINGHAM

As its subtitle suggests, this book was written with a view to encouraging honest, searching dialogue between Christians and between Jews and Christians. Its writers, under the editorship of Prof. George A. F. Knight, of McCormick Theological Seminary, Chicago, are attempting to put their Judeo-Christian faith in a way that will be conducive to and create a climate for dialogue. They were aware that to do this there could be no whittling down, minimizing, or distorting of the Christian faith for accommodation's sake. Rather, there must be a clear, unequivocally honest and forthright setting forth of the Christian position. This, the writers knew, would surely involve a serious treatment of such matters as the following chapter titles suggest: "The Peculiar Sociological Situation of the Jewish People in North America"; "The Messianic Hope"; "The Meaning of Prophecy"; and "Anti-Semitism." Beyond this, if "Preparation for Dialogue" were to have meaning other than that of a catchphrase, there must be a consideration of the image that each (Jew or Christian) holds of the other, and what each group sees as its particular advantage—theological, ethical, or existential—in relation to the culture and the thought-action patterns of contemporary man and his society. Significantly, therefore, one of the chapters of the book addresses itself to the urgent question, "Building Theological Bridges."

The reader will not progress far into the book's content without discovering that every care is taken to describe and discuss the Christian faith within the context of its Judaic roots—theological, ethical, historical. This is done in the conviction that when attempts are made to divorce Christianity from this background, Christianity has no meaning, message, or mission. It is then, at best, only an ephemeral oddity of mere passing consequence. What is more, the writers are concerned to point out the common bonds within the covenant of God that bind Jew and Christian together and relate them in a way that is utterly unique. By exploring these relationships which accent the common Biblical and theological ground on which Jew and Christian stand, it is hoped that the way will be open to mutual understanding and witness.

It is a cause for real satisfaction and joy that today's world is uncovering many evidences of Jews and Christians working together for the good of society as fellow sharers in a common humanity. Although this kind of mutuality is highly commendable, the writers of this "Preparation for Dialogue" strongly insist that there is more to the relationship than a friendly, surface-oriented desire to be do-gooders together or to be fellow sharers in a common philanthropy. Between Jews and Christians there is an interdependence, the strength and depth of which is rooted uniquely in the redemptive mission of the covenant-making God in and to his world. It is an interrelatedness, therefore, whose essence and urgency rests not on human whim or fancy, but on a common involvement of Jew and Christian in the sovereign intention of God in history.

The reader should know, too, that in the original planning for this book, another purpose loomed large. Many pastors across the church whose parishes were located in areas having a substantial Jewish minority or majority were writing in to their denominational headquarters asking for help in understanding the Christian church's relation to the Jewish people. These pastors were asking questions such as: Has the church any mission responsibility toward the Jews, and if so, what is its nature? What are the grounds and the urgency for the church's seeking a meaningful communication with the Jewish people? What should the church's attitude be toward these people? A deep need was felt for a book that would grapple with these and other pertinent questions, principally within a theological, Biblical context, not overlooking, however, the sociological and practical implications of the question. The writers aimed, therefore, at producing a text that would be useful in dialogue between Christians as well as between Jews and Christians.

Some readers of the book may wonder why the Jewish side of the case is not treated with the thoroughness accorded the Christian side. If the content is to have integrity, they say, as "Preparation for Dialogue," should not a careful balance in treatment be observed? The writers are not unaware of this concern. However, they feel that many good books by Jewish authors dealing with Jewish theology and ethics are available. Some of these volumes are particularly relevant as resource for dialogue, since they have been written with a Christian as well as a Jewish reading public in mind.

As both preparation and resource for dialogue, this book will hopefully prove useful in the discussion of such questions as: (1) What do Jews and Christians religiously have to share with each other which they can and ought to share? (2) Can there be any agreement between Jews and Christians about a legitimate witness of each to the other? (3) What is the importance or significance of Judaism for Christianity? of Christianity for Judaism? (4) Is the Christian who takes seriously the New Testament grounds for evangelism and witness justified in Jewish eyes when he includes the Jew in his mission concern? Or to put it another way, does the Jew see that the Christian who takes seriously the New Testament rationale for witness has any justification at all for a universal evangelism? (5) On what grounds can Jews and Christians enter into dialogue about Christ? (6) What has been the unintentional but effective witness impact of Judaism upon Christianity and of Christianity upon Judaism? (7) In what sense are Judaism and Christianity missionary faiths? (8) How has it come about that modern Judaism has apparently abandoned the evangelistic motivation and practice of the Judaism of New Testament times? (9) What elements of Christian theology and teaching does Judaism see as constituting the major blocks to Jewish-Christian dialogue? (10) What common theological grounds do Jews and Christians have around which they can gather for dialogue? (11) How do we distinguish between legitimate communication or proclamation of one's faith and the various forms of proselytism? (12) What are the common theological and existential convictions shared by Jews and Christians that would tend to create a favorable climate for dialogue?

It will be obvious to the reader that in this book we are not seeking either to proselytize and propagandize, or to offer a many-sided statement of the question that will leave the reader bewildered. Our intention is simply to make a plain statement of the Christian faith in relation to Judaism, and within the context of Jewish theology, history, and culture. The book is designed to meet a fourfold purpose: (1) to encourage the church to engage in Jewish-Christian dialogue; (2) to help prepare the church for such dialogue; (3) to furnish much-needed resource materials; and (4) to raise the kinds of questions that would have significance for such a dialogue.

The National Council of Churches' Committee on the Church and the Jewish People takes pleasure in commending this book, *Jews and Christians: Preparation for Dialogue* to Christian groups. Two sides of the preparation of Christians for this all-important dialogue with the Jewish community need to be held together:

1. The theological task of acknowledging the relationship of the Christian faith to the Jewish community from which it came.
2. The historical task of feeling the depth of alienation that has resulted from the long and tragic history of anti-Semitism, and of seeking to find the way across this desert of alienation by repentance and knowledge—

knowledge gained by listening to the Jew as he explains his tradition.

These two sides of the task of preparation should be pursued together. It is our hope, therefore, that this book which so ably fulfills the theological task will be studied by Christian groups along with a book such as *Our Religion and Our Neighbors,* by Milton G. Miller and Sylvan D. Schwartzman (Union of American Hebrew Congregations, 1963) and that as groups pursue this study they will invite members of the Jewish community to help them with this second task—the task of finding the way to the true repentance toward, and knowledge of, our neighbors in faith from which alone true dialogue can spring.

Chapter One

THE PECULIAR SOCIOLOGICAL SITUATION OF THE JEWISH PEOPLE IN NORTH AMERICA

The Jewish people are scattered among all the nations. The Jewish faith is one, however, and a traveler feels at home whether he enters a synagogue in Calcutta, New York, or Buenos Aires. But Jewish thinking, like Gentile thinking, is naturally affected by the environment in which it finds itself. European Jewry, for example, is unfortunately now the mere handful that has survived the holocaust. The State of Israel, again, houses a self-confident and creative people, whose views on the ultimate issues of life are unlikely to resemble those of the remnant left in Europe. American Jewry, once again, dwells in a land where men have been free, where the ghetto is unknown, and where Jews and Christians live as neighbors and as friends. It is natural, then, that an attempt at dialogue, such as this, between Jews and Christians in North America, should be prefaced, at least for the Christian reader, by a survey of the sociological factors affecting Jews in America. There are creative Jewish thinkers in North America who, in seeking to express their Judaism within this free society, reveal the effect upon Jewish thinking of the dominant Christian church and of its American theologians. Edmund F. Perry, professor at Northwestern University, Evanston, Illinois is the author of this first chapter. He has included statistical material supplied by Ovid R. Sellers, professor emeritus at McCormick Theological Seminary, Chicago.

—*The Editor*

Jews have been present and active in the New World literally from its beginning. There were Jews with Columbus when he "discovered" America in 1492, and Jews have been present here ever since, first in the colonies and then in the states.

Jewish participation in the American venture has contributed immeasurably to the shaping of the New World, and continues to do so; it has also issued in a new, distinctively *American* form of Jewry. The internal social dynamics and structures of American Jewry today are as distinctively American as is the relatively free and forceful role of the American Jewish community in the total society of America. It is this social situation within American Jewry that we are primarily concerned with in this chapter, and yet, as already suggested, the internal situation of this "little society" of Jews is part and parcel of the "big society" of America and can never be studied entirely apart from the larger social context. (The converse of that also needs to be emphasized: The social processes of the total American society can be adequately considered only when the contribution of the Jewish "little society" is reckoned with fully.)

Although Jews were present and active in the early life of the colonies, there is nothing that we can call an American Jewish community before 1654 when twenty-three Jewish refugee-immigrants from Recife, Brazil, landed and settled at New Amsterdam (later to be called New York), Holland's North American colony on the Hudson. Beginning with this small initial community, Jewry in North America has been marked by four distinct social patterns, the first three of which were determined by dominating strains in successive waves of immigrant Jews coming to America: (1) Jewry in the succession of the Sephardim, that is, Jews from Spain or Portugal or their descendants (1654–1825). (2) Reform Jewry of the Ashkenazim, that is, Jews from Germany and their descendants (1815–1900). (3) Intense religiopolitical Jewry of the East European immigrants (1880–1920). (4) Americanized Jewry. It should be noted that the overlap in dates for the first three periods is neither an error nor an inconsequential matter. There were, indeed, in each period representatives and influences from Jews other than those dominating at that time, and each successive period was in no little measure shaped by its predecessor(s). Thus contemporary American Jewry in any of its aspects cannot be understood without knowledge of the developments that took place here beginning in 1654.

We properly turn, first of all, to review in this essay the constitution of the American-Jewish community through three sociologically distinct migrations.

I. The First Jewish People in North America

The arrival at New Amsterdam of those twenty-three refugees from Brazil linked American Jews to world Jewry, and that link has never been broken since. That original link reaches back at least to 1492. In the same year that Spain sponsored Columbus' "world-making" voyage, she also initiated a reign of terror upon her populous and wealthy Jewish community. Five years later Portugal began expulsion of her Jews.

Many found sanctuary in the countries around the Mediterranean. Some settled secretly in the forbidden countries and particularly in the colonies of the New World. It was in Amsterdam, Holland, that the largest and most prosperous group settled. And this group enjoyed a high degree of freedom.

In 1631 the Dutch wrested Recife, the capital of Brazil, from the Portuguese. Then in Recife as in Amsterdam, the Jews were permitted unrestricted activity and began openly to profess and practice their faith. Soon they were joined by other Sephardic immigrants from Holland.

Freedom for Jews in Recife was short-lived. In 1654 the Portuguese recaptured their capital and unleashed persecution upon the Jews. Forced again to flee the Portuguese, some of the refugees found asylum in the Dutch Caribbean colonies, others returned to Amsterdam, and twenty-three settled at New Amsterdam on the Hudson.

The directors of the Dutch West India Company ruled that the Jews should be allowed to stay and trade at New Amsterdam. Stuyvesant, the director-general, however, tried to deny the immigrants full citizenship rights by imposing upon them the necessity of caring for their own poor and prohibiting them from participating in any defense of the colony. The Jews were willing and ready to assume care of their own poor but they would not agree to abstain from defending the colony, and by many letters they appealed their case to Amsterdam. They were again sustained. Amsterdam granted them all rights to participate in defense of the colony and, in addition, granted them freedom to practice their religion publicly in the colony.

Subsequent to the New Amsterdam affair, Jews arrived in other colonies. Their lot varied from one colony to another. Whereas the Puritans of Massachusetts acknowledged the Old Testament as the source of much of their ethos and ethic, they did not acknowledge any responsibility for the care and friendship of Jews, and so denied Jews permission for permanent residence. In both Virginia and Maryland, Jews were excluded for religious reasons. Newport, Rhode Island, welcomed a group of Jews shortly after the New Amsterdam affair. In South Carolina, Jews were granted right of residence, ownership of property, and freedom to build a synagogue. Georgia also admitted Jews and acknowledged their right to build a synagogue.

Having opened a door of entrance to North America, Sephardic Jews continued to stream in by way of Brazil, the Caribbean islands, Holland, and England, while some came directly from Spain or Portugal. These Sephardim were joined during these early days by small numbers of Jews from Germany and Poland, but it was the Sephardic strain that characterized Judaism in the New World until about 1825.

In Europe the Sephardic and Ashkenazic communities had maintained rigid separation. There the religious ritual did not differ greatly in detail, but the Sephardim maintained a feeling of cultural aristocracy and refused to associate with the poorer, more uncouth European Jews. In America, however, the Sephardim accepted the Ashkenazim with little self-consciousness on the part of either.

Neither the Spanish nor the European Jews settling in colonial America were learned. In 1773 there were only three rabbis in the entire New World and they were all in the Caribbean. It was the cantor (*ḥazzan*) in the American Sephardic scene who became the Jewish counterpart of the Protestant minister, preaching sermons and teaching the children.

In the total American community a Jew was generally regarded as just another citizen, and ordinarily he participated individually in the civic, social, and political life of the larger community. As for their religion, the Jews were considered to be more or less just another dissenting sect and so were largely ignored by the civil authorities and undisturbed by the general citizenry. In a word, outside the synagogue the Jew was just another American.

II. Reform Judaism in America

Mass immigration of Jews to colonial America followed closely upon the end of the wars in Europe in 1815. The first throng of new immigrants were poor traders from Germany. Their predecessors had been German Jewish merchants who had easily identified with the Americanized Sephardim. The arrival of the traders created a class consciousness and class distinction in intra-Jewish relationships. The lower-class Ashkenazim were shocked by the snobbish attitudes of the old-timers. Frustrated and irritated by their outcast status, the newcomers enlarged the rift by criticizing the Sephardim and forming new congregations—numerous and largely German Ashkenazic.

By the 1840's another class of Jews appeared among the continuing immigration from Germany. Intellectuals, men of culture, rabbis, and political liberals were now arriving and they presented a new and strange face among Jewish immigrants. The traders and peddlers had been meticulous in their keeping of the daily Jewish practices. The intellectual immigrants were families of the German world, cultured people who had come to terms with modernity and who had been strongly influenced by the Reform movement in German Judaism.

The German Reform was a movement of organized discontent with traditional Jewish services. It included both laymen and rabbis who wanted to update both the form and content of Jewish worship. They asked for a Judaism relevant to their German social existence. In addition to new types of services, sermons were introduced in the regular weekly ritual of some synagogues. Study of the Bible and the Talmud, characteristic of traditional Jewish education, was superseded with parochial-type schools presenting a curriculum of moral instruction adjusted to the age levels of the children. The rite of *Bar Mitzvah* (a ceremony in which the Jewish boy passes from childhood to adult responsibility for the Commandments) was replaced with a confirmation ceremony for those boys and girls who could demonstrate a minimum mastery of moral education.

In effect, the Reform in German Judaism launched an attack upon the authority of tradition and the whole structure of Jewish law. Some Reformers clung to the authority of Scripture alone, but others held that critical Biblical scholarship had undermined the divine authority even of the Bible and revealed the relativity (undesirability!) of much Biblical law. Consequently, the study of the Torah was no longer set in the context of divine revelation but was understood to be a part of man's spiritual evolution, the Law itself an example of his spiritual development. The legal and ritual portions of the Bible could be neglected in this approach, and the prophetic call to social responsibility could be exalted.

It is difficult to imagine a more congenial preparation for Reform Judaism than that awaiting the rabbis arriving in the 1840's. And it is equally difficult to imagine a more dedicated or better equipped corps of Reforming rabbis. Their genius is epitomized in the person of Isaac Mayer Wise (1819–1900), who arrived in America in 1846. Wise came to this country from Bohemia to accept responsibility for a congregation in Albany, New York. His conflict with the conservative element in that synagogue was so immediate and bitter that he was attacked bodily in his pulpit. Christian friends of Wise, who included justices of the New York Supreme Court, advised him to take up law and forget the rabbinate, predicting that his liberal ideas would only meet with greater opposition. Wise did not accept his friends' invitation; instead, he accepted a call to a congregation in Cincinnati, which offered a medium for the development and dissemination of his interpretation of Judaism.

Wise paced his fellow Reform rabbis by preaching and writing in English while they were still using German. He established an English Jewish weekly, *The American Israelite,* to be his voice of Reform to American Jews: yet because German was still the language of such a large number of recent immigrants, he published a weekly in German.

Wise pursued a threefold scheme of organization to establish Reform among American Jews: (1) In 1873, with the encouragement voiced through several rabbinical conferences, Wise founded the Union of American Hebrew Congregations, a union that literally gave organizational embodiment in the United States to the Reform movement. (2) In 1875 he opened Hebrew Union College in Cincinnati, a Jewish school of higher education adapted to the needs of rabbis for American Jewry. (3) In 1889 he masterminded the formation of the Central Conference of American Rabbis, nothing less than a professional society for Reform rabbis in this country.

Rejecting the notion that the Jews had been exiled from Palestine because of their sins, the Reformers espoused the claim that God had scattered them among the nations as a part of his plan of salvation for all mankind. They remained a separate religion because destiny had assigned them the mission of instructing the nations spiritually.

David Einhorn, who sought for a sound theoretical foundation for the Reform movement, subscribed to this latter rationale, believing it to be based upon passages in Isaiah. He propagated it in America and forged it into a statement which a group of Reform rabbis in the eastern part of the nation issued as an announcement of their stand. Meeting in Philadelphia in 1869, these rabbis declared: (1) that the Messianic purpose and aim of Israel, extending through the generations of Jews, is the union of all the children of God rather than the restoration of a Jewish nation, and (2) that the Jewish state had been destroyed to further the divine purpose of instructing the nations spiritually through the Jewish religion rather than to punish Israel for disobedience.

Einhorn's efforts to reconstitute Judaism in its American version were crowned with success in 1885 when a group of rabbis meeting in Pittsburgh adopted and published the Pittsburgh Platform. Einhorn was deceased by this time, but his son-in-law, Kaufmann Kohler, continued the fight and within a few years the whole Reform rabbinate of the United States adopted the Pittsburgh declaration. The principles set forth in this statement are far more radical than any reinterpretation of Judaism suggested in Germany. The entire declaration is reprinted here.

First, we recognize in every religion an attempt to grasp the Infinite One, and in every mode, source or book of revelation held sacred in any religious system the consciousness of the indwelling of God in man. We hold that Judaism presents the highest conception of the God-idea as taught in our holy Scriptures and developed and spiritualized by the Jewish teachers in accordance with the moral and philosophical progress of their respective ages. We maintain that Judaism preserved and defended, amid continual struggles and trials and under enforced isolation, this God-idea as the central religious truth for the human race.

Second, we recognize in the Bible the record of the consecration of the Jewish people to its mission as the priest of the One God, and value it as the most potent instrument of religious and moral instruction. We hold that the modern discoveries of scientific researches in the domains of nature and history are not antagonistic to the doctrines of Judaism, the Bible reflecting the primitive ideas of its own age and dealing with man in miraculous narratives.

Third, we recognize in the Mosaic legislation a system of training the Jewish people for its mission during its national life in Palestine, and today we accept as binding only its moral laws and maintain only such ceremonials as elevate and sanctify our lives, but reject all such as are not adapted to the views and habits of modern civilization.

Fourth, we hold that all such Mosaic and Rabbinical laws as regulate diet, priestly purity and dress originated in ages and under the influence of ideas altogether foreign to our present mental and spiritual state. They fail to impress the modern Jew with a spirit of priestly holiness; their observance in our day is apt rather to obstruct than to further modern spiritual elevation.

Fifth, we recognize in the modern era of universal culture of heart and intellect the approach of the realization of Israel's great Messianic hope for the establishment of the Kingdom of truth, justice and peace among all men. We consider ourselves no longer a nation but a religious community, and therefore expect neither a return to Palestine, nor a sacrificial worship under the administration of the sons of Aaron, nor the restoration of any of the laws concerning the Jewish state.

Sixth, we recognize in Judaism a progressive religion, ever striving to be in accord with the postulates of reason. We are convinced of the utmost necessity of preserving the historical identity with our great past. Christianity and Islam being daughter religions of Judaism, we appreciate their mission to aid in the spreading of monotheistic and moral truth. We acknowledge that the spirit of broad humanity of our age is our ally in the fulfillment of our mission, and therefore we extend the hand of fellowship to all who co-operate with us in the establishment of the reign of truth and righteousness among men.

Seventh, we reassert the doctrine of Judaism, that the soul of man is immortal, grounding this belief on the divine nature of the human spirit, which forever finds bliss in righteousness and misery in wickedness. We reject as ideas not rooted in Judaism the belief both in bodily resurrection and in Gehenna and Eden (hell and paradise), as abodes for everlasting punishment or reward.

Eighth, in full accordance with the spirit of Mosaic legislation which strives to regulate the relation between rich and poor, we deem it our duty to participate in the great task of modern times, to solve on the basis of justice and righteousness the problems presented by the contrasts and evils of the present organization of society.

Elements in this Platform strike the Christian reader as radical departures from the Biblical heritage of the Jew. The Christian believes that he sees here the substitution of the idea of the evolution of religion for an acceptance of the divine election; a rather Platonic separation between soul and body; and the supremacy of human reason over divine revelation—yet, of course, the church of the same period was also playing with just such liberal ideas.

Reform Judaism had now unquestionably become the definer of Judaism in America and by its definitions both the Sephardic and dissenting Ashkenazic Jews were made to be "conservers" of traditional teaching and practice. The antitraditional, antinationalistic emphasis of the Reform was consummated in something of a grand finale in 1894 when its rabbis and congregations published a *Union Prayerbook* in which Hebrew was almost totally eliminated. Furthermore, all references to the restoration of the Temple, all references to the exile as punishment, all prayers to God to rebuild Jerusalem and to bring the Jewish people together again in the land of Israel—all these were omitted from the new prayerbook. The individualization of religion had reached its climax. "What I think is really what ultimately matters!"

There were several aspects of Reform, however, that were not as logical as the vague universalism and rugged individualism just cited. Intermarriage between Jews and non-Jews was vigorously discouraged by Reformers whose attitude otherwise was "the more we get together the happier we'll be." On the other hand, the Central Conference of American Rabbis abandoned the requirement of circumcision for male converts but continued to require it for males born to Jewish families.

These apparent inconsistencies in the rationalizations of Reform suggest a tenacious attachment, perhaps unconscious, to the Jewish "people." At any rate, in 1937, confronted by the grim prospect of Hitler's anti-Jewish measures, the Reform rabbinate met in Columbus, Ohio, and drafted a statement that superseded the Pittsburgh Platform. The classic Reform principle—that Judaism is a progressive religion—was preserved. The revolutionary twist in the new statement came in Sections 4 and 5. Section 4, headed "Torah," asserted that "certain . . . laws have lost their binding force with the passing of the conditions that called them forth," but added that as "a depository of permanent spiritual ideals, the Torah remains the dynamic source of the life of Israel." Section 5 began with the Reform party line and then reversed the Pittsburgh principle that had reduced Judaism from a people to a religion only:

> Judaism is the soul of which Israel is the body. Living in all parts of the world, Israel has been held together by the ties of a common history, and above all by the heritage of the faith. Though we recognize in the group-loyalty of Jews who have become estranged from our religious tradition a bond that still unites them with us, we maintain that it is by its religion and for its religion that the Jewish people has lived. The non-Jew who accepts our faith is welcome as a full member of the Jewish community.
>
> In all lands where our people live, they assume and seek to share loyally the full duties and responsibilities of citizenship and to create seats of Jewish knowledge and religion. In the rehabilitation of Palestine, the land hallowed by memories and hopes, we behold the promise of a renewed life for many of our brethren. We affirm the obligation of all Jewry to aid in its upbuilding as a Jewish homeland by endeavoring to make it not only a refuge for the oppressed but also a center of Jewish culture and spiritual life.

It was difficult to predict in 1937 whether the Reform rabbinate and congregations would make further readmissions of traditional Jewish belief and practice into their movement. But let us now consider the shape and force of the Conservative movement which developed primarily in reaction to the Reform, and let us also introduce the Orthodox Judaism which moved in temporarily to dwarf both Conservatism and Reform.

III. The Contribution of East European Orthodoxy

The Conservative protest against Reform was more vocal than numerical. In 1887 when Conservative rabbis launched the Jewish Theological Seminary in New York for the purpose of training non-Reform rabbis in America, only eleven congregations in the entire country supported the enterprise. At the forefront of these eleven were the old Sephardic synagogues of New York and Philadelphia.

The Conservative rationale was set forth succinctly in the preamble to the constitution of the association formed to support the new seminary:

> The necessity has been made manifest for associated and organized effort on the part of the Jews of America faithful to Mosaic Law and ancestral traditions, for the purpose of keeping alive the true Judaic spirit; in particular by the establishment of a seminary where the Bible shall be impartially taught and rabbinical literature faithfully expounded, and more especially where youths, desirous of entering the ministry, may be thoroughly grounded in Jewish knowledge and inspired by the precept and example of their instructors with the love of the Hebrew language and a spirit of devotion and fidelity to the Jewish law.

The authority of Scripture and tradition is asserted here; the primacy and supremacy of Mosaic law is confessed, and the indispensability of the Hebrew language for the life of faith and learning is claimed.

Conservatism could not stem the tide of Reform. In fact, by 1900 six of the original eleven congregations supporting the new seminary had affiliated with the Reform!

Reform was checked by the influx of East European Jewish immigrants inundating the American Jewish scene between 1880 and 1920. In 1880 there were 250,000 Jews in America, the vast majority of whom were identified with the Reform. By 1900 a half million East European Jews were in this country, clearly here to stay and clearly having no affinity for Reform. By 1920 the new group's ranks had increased to 1,750,000. The Reform was now a minority social elite.

On arrival the new immigrants found two areas of employment, peddling and the needle trades in factories, and took up residence in slums. They were industrious and ambitious, and so by 1927 many of the first-generation East Europeans had greatly improved their lot financially in the trades and many had become small shopkeepers and small-business owners. The second generation boasted a high school education, many a college degree, and still others professional and graduate training. This second generation were to be found working as bookkeepers, accountants, salesmen, clerks, and a few in law, medicine, and other professions. Both first- and second-generation immigrants were moving out of the slums into areas of second settlement, which offered middle-class apartments or duplexes, occasionally modest single-family dwellings. Some joined older Jewish Americans in moving to areas of third settlement, that is, to expensive apartment houses and suburban developments of single-family houses.

The employment and residence situation in America soon modified the insularity of the East Europeans' religion. The Conservative leadership saw an opportunity both to brake the influence of Reform and to serve the newly arrived Jewish constituency. The faltering, floundering Jewish Theological Seminary in New York was reorganized to educate rabbis for the masses of new American Jewish citizens. For the record, it must be related that a Reform Jew, one Jacob Schiff, put up the money for the reconstitution of the Seminary!

The young rabbinate graduates, themselves the sons of the new immigrants, were not acceptable to the congregations originally formed by East Europeans. Consequently, these young ministers would take an older congregation and work to attract their fellow immigrants into its membership. The result was a new conservatism, neither primarily a reaction to Reform nor yet a carbon copy of East European Orthodoxy. In 1913, sixteen of these Conservative congregations formed the United Synagogue of America.

Except for the slum areas where only the poverty-stricken East Europeans remained, every expression of Judaism in this country had become "Americanized" by the time of the post First World War period. In the slum areas, kosher markets and restaurants struggled along; religious schools for children operated both an all-day and an afternoon session. The synagogues were Orthodox, and the service was conducted in Hebrew. It is here in the slums that we leave Old World Judaism and turn to the fourth stage of Judaism in America, which is Americanized Judaism in its present expression.

IV. Americanized Jewry

In the late 1920's, Orthodoxy of the East European variety continued to dominate the synagogues but not the Jews in the area of second settlement (middle-class apartments, two-family units, sometimes a single-family dwelling). The greatest number of American Jews were to be found here, the greatest change in economic status was represented here, the most democratic amalgam of the several Jewish migrations was present here, and the largest number of synagogue buildings were constructed here. The religion of the synagogues was predominantly a modified orthodoxy because the majority of the population in these areas was of the East European strain. The sermons were in English, however, and the service was rather formal. Some congregations in these areas identified with the Conservative, and occasionally a Reform temple remained to recall the days when German Jews occupied the entire area.

Although Jewish children in large numbers were attending synagogue schools in second-settlement areas, they were not being trained in Jewish life. By now it was widely assumed that Jewish life was not dependent upon Jewish religion, and polls taken during this period indicated that the synagogue's influence upon individuals and the community was negligible. Jewish philanthropic, defense, and benevolent societies increased rapidly and commanded the energies of the majority of Jews. It seemed to the majority that Jewish life was best expressed in social action: support of Jewish hospitals, orphanages, old people's homes, settlement houses, social agencies for the poor, fund-raising for Jews in Europe, and enlargement of the variety of Zionist agencies.

Between the end of World War I and 1939, Jews of every variety of persuasion were convinced that Judaism could become American. Immigration laws that were passed in 1921, 1924, and 1929 shut off "the supply line" from Europe, and American Jewry came under the leadership of second-generation, American-born Jews. "In their competition with each other," Moshe Davis writes, "all the religious groups soon discovered that each was emphasizing the same ideals for a healthy Jewish life in America: learning, scholarship, traditional values and ceremonials, the influence of Eretz Yisrael, ethical and social objectives." (Pp. 548 ff., *The Jews: Their History, Culture, and Religion*, edited by Louis Finkelstein, 3d ed., 2 vols; Harper & Row, Publishers, Inc., 1960.)

This unity which was dimly seen in the blast of their competition became a reality with the outbreak of World War II. The American rabbinate had to prepare to take care of the half million young Jewish men and women who were to serve in the Armed Forces of their country. Harmony among the several groups resulted in the production and distribution of liturgical materials, of literature and guides for adapting Jewish life to military service. This necessity of cooperating to meet Jewish needs in the national emergency set the precedent for postwar years when Reform, Conservative, and Orthodox rabbis and congregations involved themselves in a series of coordinating meetings. Across their denominational lines, Jews began to work together in the larger community to consider the issue of "separateness," "religion," and "peoplehood." For a long time there had been "dejudaized Jews" who were prepared to give up all Jewish identity and separateness. For example, in 1946, the distinguished Arthur Koestler wrote in *The New York Times:*

> I am in favor of Jews becoming assimilated with and absorbed by the countries in which they live. I think it is high time to liquidate this anachronism of a separate community all over the world, which cannot be defined as a separate race, or nation, or religious sect and whose insistence on remaining in one way apart has led to an unparalleled chain of massacres, persecutions and expulsions for 1500 years.

When the new State of Israel was created in 1948, American Jews had forced upon them in a most practical way the question of what form of Jewish separateness, if any, should be maintained by Jews outside of Israel. Mr. Koestler spoke to the issue again in *Promise and Fulfillment: Palestine, 1917–1949* (The Macmillan Company, 1949), pp. 232–235:

> The existence of the Hebrew state—that is, the State whose language and culture are Hebrew, not Yiddish, Polish or American—puts every Jew outside of Israel before a dilemma which will become increasingly acute. It is the choice between becoming a citizen of the Hebrew nation and renouncing any conscious or implicit claim to separate nationhood.
>
> To break the vicious circle of being persecuted for being "different," and being "different" by force of persecution, they must arrive at a clear decision, however difficult this may be. They must either follow the imperative of their religion and return to the promised land—*or recognize that that faith is no longer theirs.* To renounce the Jewish faith does not mean to jetison the perennial values of Judaic tradition. Its essential teachings have passed long ago into the mainstream of the Judeo-Christian heritage. If a Judaic religion is to survive outside Israel, without inflicting the stigma of separateness on its followers and

laying them open to the charge of divided loyalty, it would have to be a system of faith and cosmopolitan ethics freed from all racial presumption and national exclusivity. *But a Jewish religion thus reformed would be stripped of all its specifically Jewish content.* [Italics in this paragraph were added.]

Mr. Koestler apparently asked for nothing less than that all Jews electing to stay in America elect for themselves some other badge of religious identity than that of Judaism. Yet reaction to Mr. Koestler's interpretation of the decision before American Jewry was strong and direct, suggesting that his interpretation represented far more than the private and individualistic opinion of one man.

The vast majority of American Jews, for varying reasons, have elected to remain in America with kind dispositions and generous actions toward the State of Israel and its citizens. What is happening to and among these American Jews?

In 1961 the estimated number of Jews in the United States was 5,500,000, slightly over 3 percent; and in Canada, 275,000, a little more than 5 percent of the entire population. The largest percentage of Jews is in urban centers; according to the 1962 *American Jewish Year Book,* in the State of New York the percentage of Jews is 14.5; in the District of Columbia, 5.3; in Massachusetts, 4.29; in Pennsylvania, 3.96; in Connecticut, 3.92; in California, 3.49; in Illinois, 2.90. In rural states with no large cities, the percentage of Jews is small. In Arkansas it is 0.15; in Montana, 0.09; in Idaho, 0.08. The Jews in Canada are concentrated in the large cities—Montreal, Toronto, Winnipeg, and Vancouver.

The most dramatic aspect of present-day American Judaism is its at-homeness in the suburbs. Within one decade (1948–1958), twelve million Americans moved to the suburbs, mostly from the large cities, and today around fifty million people live in suburbia. Heretofore, migration from the cities was "the way" of those wanting to escape the minorities, but especially since the end of World War II the minorities have participated in the move to suburbia. Jews are no exception to this phenomenon. Two thirds, or 3,700,000, of America's

5,500,000 Jews live in or adjacent to ten large U.S. cities. Studies such as Albert Gordon's *Jews in Suburbia* vividly detail for the general as well as the research reader the status and trends of Jewish life in the American suburbs. In terms of economics, community problems, education, and politics, the Jews in suburbia show no significant distinctions from their Protestant and Roman Catholic neighbors. And in religion they are expected by their neighbors to be "something." That is one of the requirements of the "suburban way of life." So, as Will Herberg indicates in his *Protestant—Catholic—Jew,* Judaism has become a badge of identification. But this suburban pressure to identify in terms of religion is at least a first step toward a reaffirmation of Judaism, or so Gordon's studies indicate. Other factors tend to move the Jew farther toward his religious roots. Jewish children play with Christian children in the suburbs, and they go to school together. Christian children inquire of their Jewish playmates: "What is a Jew? Where do you go to church?" Almost universally these questions are asked in innocence and good spirit. (Name-calling and intergroup fighting are frowned upon in the suburbs.) The Jewish settlers find religious questions impinging upon their consciousness. For when the child asks his parents why he is a Jew and what makes him so, the parents confess to rabbis and social researchers that they do not have the answers, either because they have had no Jewish education or because the Jewish education they had did not equip them to answer questions of faith identity.

Such circumstances as just outlined have sent parents in search of rabbis, and rabbis in search of a new form of Jewish education. The suburban synagogue, like the suburban home, regardless of religion, has become child-centered. Judaism is being re-created for the children: increasingly, significant roles are given to children in the service, religious festivals are recast so as to glorify Jewish life for children, and the children are permitted to invite their Christian playmates to special occasions at home and at the synagogue.

The life of the adult Jew in suburbia is not as fully integrated into the total community as is that of his children. To be sure, Christians and Jews are friendly; they work together in the P.T.A., in precinct politics, on the United Fund campaigns. In connection with these civic services they may "party" together, but on a week-after-week basis there is little social life for the suburban Jew outside of Jewish circles. This very fact itself has brought many Jews into closer association with the suburban synagogue and Jewish center, for needing social life, most Jews were easy captives for the energetic and aggressive upholders of Jewish religion and religious institutions.

The social studies already mentioned point to a genuine and growing concern of suburban Jews for religion—religion for themselves, for their children, and for "de-judaized Jews." It is now generally conceded that the story of Judaism in America is the story of the disintegration of an entire way of life, perhaps three ways of life. And few Jews, well-informed or otherwise, want a return to what is now gone. Reform, Conservatism, Orthodoxy—these and other former "ways" are no longer a way at all for American Jewry. But there is a widespread, authentic demand now for a distinctively Jewish style of living for Jews in America.

What this new style will be, none of us, of course, can say. Yet the object of this volume is to declare, from the Christian angle, that the church has a great responsibility for the future of Jewry in North America. For it is an undeniable fact that the Jewish people will find their ultimate way only in fellowship with and juxtaposition to Christian belief and practice.

Chapter Two

THE "MYSTERY" OF ISRAEL

The Christian church claims to be "Israel." The Jewish people, naturally, *is* Israel. These two statements, which appear to be quite irreconcilable, reveal the imperative need for an honest and open expression of views—indeed, for a true dialogue between Jews and Christians.

This chapter expresses one side of the dialogue only. Jewish theologians have already expressed their understanding of this issue in recent volumes. Dialogue ought not to read as an intransigent expression of the views of one side in a controversy, and Christian readers of these Jewish works have not found them so. Let the Jewish reader, therefore, see this chapter in a similar light. Let him recognize it to be the statement of a deeply held position of those who see the "mystery" of Israel in the light of the New Testament. Let neither Jew nor Christian search for some "Lowest Common Denominator" about which they could agree without controversy. Rather, let each, in thoughtful and humble dialogue, express his own unique "Highest Common Factor" as he sees it. The chapter is by the Editor of the volume.

—*The Editor*

Both Jews and Christians are deeply aware of the mystery of Israel's existence in our midst. This awareness is revealed when the Christian asks the Jew the old question, to which the Jew struggles to give an adequate reply, viz., "What is a

Jew?" It is not our task in this volume, however, to attempt a secular explanation of the mystery of Israel, whether in terms of ethnology or of politics. Our task is to seek to state the Biblical and theological answer to the question given above. To that end, therefore, this chapter handles the issue under five heads.

I. The Mystery of the Covenant

It is obvious, in the first place, that Israel is unique among the peoples of the world in being the People of the Covenant. For Israel is that people with whom God has continued in a special relationship for more than three thousand years, in fact, ever since the early Bronze Age in the development of human civilization. Throughout all that immensely long period, Israel has been "in covenant" with the living God! This extraordinary idea must surely claim our attention.

We read first of a covenant that God makes with all humanity in and through his servant Noah (Gen. 6:18). This covenant was aimed at including all Noah's descendants along with him (ch. 9:9), and even all the living creatures on the earth (v. 10). That is to say, the early theologians of Israel believed that their God sought to bind himself to his creatures in a living relationship, and was not, therefore, to remain remote and completely unknown by man, who is made in his image. Second, we read how, from out of all the peoples of the earth, God selects one man, viz., Abraham, for the advancement of his purpose. This purpose is now to go forward, in fact, by means of the special relationship of covenant, for God by this act establishes a covenant between himself and all Abraham's descendants, in order that all mankind may benefit thereby (ch. 12:1–3). Later on, Abraham is re-called to be the "father" of the People of Israel (cf. Isa. 51:2), and this special relationship is then specifically deemed a covenant (Lev. 26:42). Then note that the promise which God gives to Abraham at the creation of this covenant is renewed at a later date. This is when the birth of Isaac as a child of faith is promised. Moreover, it is only then, at the moment when the grace of God becomes clearly manifest, that the word "covenant" is specifically employed in Genesis to describe the relationship that has come into being between God and the line of ancient patriarchs (Gen. 17:19). Moreover, God now declares that he will never break this covenant (ch. 17:2 ff.). Thus, when God's promises are renewed, first to Isaac (ch. 26:1–5) and then to Jacob (ch. 28:10–17, etc.), the reader understands how the covenant is bound to stand in days to come, since he has now seen it renewed with each of the first three generations.

One aspect of the divine covenant in the Old Testament is God's promise that Israel's descendants will multiply in number as the stars of the sky. Accordingly, after a long period of service in Egypt, we read how Israel does indeed do this very thing, so that when Moses leads forth his people out of slavery, it is a great multitude that reaches the wilderness across the Red Sea. Yet immediately thereafter, at the foot of Mt. Sinai, God next offers Israel through Moses a new fullness of covenant fellowship. This time, moreover, the offer is not to the people "in embryo," so to speak, if we consider the patriarchs to be such, but to the nation as she has now multiplied in terms of the promise. For God has thus far kept his promise. We read of the terms of the new offer in these words: "If you will obey my voice and keep my covenant, you shall be my own possession among all peoples; for all the earth is mine, and you shall be to me a kingdom of priests and a holy nation" (Ex. 19:5–6).

A few words of exposition are in order, first, of the phrase "my own possession." An Eastern king, of course, owned the whole land within the boundaries of his realm. He was, therefore, virtually lord of every homestead, farm, and workshop in all the land. Yet it was only when he let the jewels which he kept within his treasure chest in his palace run through his fingers that he found any real and abiding satisfaction. Now, the words "my own possession," which we read above, refer to just such a treasure chest as an ancient king possessed. The verse means, therefore, that while God indeed "possesses" all the nations of mankind, so that all men are his children, yet Israel is peculiarly near to God's own heart. For Israel is no less than God's "firstborn son" (Ex. 4:22), and the firstborn in an Eastern home is always deemed the "beloved." (In fact, the Septuagint regularly translates the Hebrew for "only" son into the Greek for "beloved.")

Secondly, let us look at the phrase "a kingdom of priests," as it is used of Israel. Now, a priest is one who is not called primarily to minister to himself, but is there to serve God and his fellowmen. Israel therefore, as a "royal priesthood," is to be a company of priests under God their king; and they are called, not for their own sake, but for the sake of the peoples of the earth. The end that God has in view, therefore, when he enters into covenant with Israel, is not to be the "election" of Israel to salvation, and the consequent neglect, or even the damnation, of all the rest! The significance of God's election of Israel rests upon the need of the world.

It is actually to meet this need, in fact, that Israel is called in covenant to be the instrument that God purposes to use. That is why Israel is called to be a "holy nation," as well as a kingdom of priests. This word "holy," again, in its earliest usages, meant "to be separated off," and so to be separated from all that is evil and sinful. Consequently, it meant also the obverse of separation from evil, for it meant to be separated off *to* God, and so to belong within the sphere of God's ongoing plan. Now, the word used here for "nation" is the Hebrew word *goy*, a word that is applied to the multitudes of humanity upon the earth, even as they form themselves into responsible groupings. Therefore, its use here means that Israel actually begins her calling even while she is still an ordinary nation among the other nations of the earth.

In later centuries, however, the great prophets of Israel sought to interpret the extraordinary phenomenon of the Sinai covenant by the use of various metaphors. One such was to liken it to a marriage covenant that was made between God and Israel. That is why we normally refer to Israel as "she." It was Hosea who first employed this amazing figure. He actually dared to call the living God the divine husband of Israel. Jeremiah, Ezekiel, and Second Isaiah all followed Hosea in this regard, and all continued to use the figure over the period of a couple of centuries. These prophets, however, preferred to use the noun *'am* for Israel as a people, and normally reserved the term *goy* for what we translate as Gentile. The other nations, therefore, we note, continue to be *goyim,* even as Israel was a *goy* when first elected, that is to say, they were normal, natural, human, political units. But Israel is something special in God's sight, and so cannot continue to be termed a mere *goy;* for Israel is, in fact, married to the Lord. These same prophets, again, like to employ the Hebrew noun *ḥesed* to describe (if that could ever be possible) the content of this unique marriage covenant relationship. In a word, we might say that on God's part this noun means something like "O love that wilt not let me go." For this strange word covers a wide range of ideas that need many words to express them in English; it speaks of covenant love, covenant loyalty, covenant devotion, convenant mercy, covenant loving-kindness, and even more. So Israel is *the* people of God in a very special sense, and under no circumstances whatsoever will God ever break his covenant with her. Since God does not change, and is always the faithful God, so his promise, his plighted troth, will never waver either.

At a later date, Second Isaiah in particular refers to the purpose or end that God has in view and which he means to attain through this covenant relationship with Israel. His argument is that the covenant is not merely for Israel's good; it is for the sake of the nations of the world. Israel, in fact, stands in the unique relationship to God that she does, in order to "bring forth justice to the nations" (Isa. 42:1). Thus Second Isaiah can also declare on God's behalf, "I have given you as a covenant to the people [of the earth], a light to the nations" (ch. 42:6), "that my salvation may reach to the end of the earth" (ch. 49:6).

In the above brief sketch, then, we see how God's love for covenant-making grew ever more clear in Israel's story, and how the object of his election, as the instrument of his purpose, was ever more carefully defined.

II. The Name "Israel"

The second element in the mystery of Israel is the very name "Israel" itself. For the word is used in a number of ways both in the Bible and at the present day. First, Israel is the new name that Jacob receives once he has wrestled all night with the spirit of God or an angel of God, and once (could we say?) he has been "converted." The ancient Hebrew world liked to give a man a name that fully described its owner. That is why, when Jacob the "heel" (to use the modern English slang) becomes "a new man" at his conversion, he receives at the same time a new name to describe him. For the name "Israel" was popularly believed to mean "God strives," or else "strong with God." Thus Israel is now the name of the new, forgiven man, the man whom God is pointing to as the one he can use for his plan.

Secondly, Israel is the name of that whole people which is descended from this their eponymous ancestor. We notice that when the prophets want to emphasize, on the one hand, this people's recalcitrant nature, they like to call them "Jacob"; but when, on the other hand, the emphasis is upon the grace of God and upon his loving purpose for a people that is wholly dependent upon God alone, the prophets normally use the name "Israel."

Thirdly, for a period of almost exactly two hundred years the name "Israel" was employed as the collective name of those same Northern tribes that broke off from the Davidic rule after the death of Solomon; the South consequently had then to be known by the name of their predominant tribe, Judah. But that the name "Israel" persisted with respect even to the Southern people we see from Isa. 5:7; Micah 3:1; etc. But after 721 B.C., when the Northern nation was finally overwhelmed by the Assyrian empire, and ceased to be a viable entity as a people in their own right, the name "Israel," almost at once, again became the name of the "ideal" People of God, whether that people was living in exile or was safe in the city of David.

Fourthly, the name has been used until the present day for the Jewish people as a whole, particularly when the emphasis is wont to be laid upon their election as the People of God, and when they are thought of as having theological significance rather than as being merely a particular ethnic group. Thus, Judah Hallevi (1085–1140), of Toledo, in his *Khuzari* (i, 115; iv, 23) emphasized that Israel is not an *ethnos*. "One word," he declared, could "free" the Jewish believer from the "yoke of the Law." That "one word" was confession of another religion. (It was only during the past century that the "racist theory" grew up on the continent of Europe.) The Jew who did not regard himself as part of Israel, the People of God, was therefore only a Jehudi.

Fifthly, when the Zionists reconstituted that particular area of their ancient homeland which they had won in their struggle against the Arabs—that territory which they were holding at the moment of the armistice that was entered into in May, 1948—they called it by the name of "Israel." For, of course, the word "Palestine" means in reality "the land of the Philistines." Naturally, it would be intolerable for the modern Zionist to call the ancient land of the people of Israel by such a name.

Finally, Israel has become the liturgical name for the Christian church. Each local congregation, in fact, sees itself as Israel, and week by week makes pilgrimage up Zion's hill, singing as it goes the ancient psalms of the People of God. Thus the church believes that it has entered into a continuity of divine activity that began with the promises made to Abraham, that continued through the whole period of the Old Testament covenant with Israel, including that of the kings with whom God had made a special covenant, and on through Christ, who was himself the summation of Israel as well as her King, till every nation under the sun finds itself represented in the people of God because of the transforming power of Jesus Christ their King. For, empowered by him, it is the church that now seeks to be a light to the nations, "that my salvation may reach to the end of the earth." It is the church, when it remembers to be the church, that knows an inner compulsion to go forth into the highways and hedges and "compel them to come in"; and so it is the church (thus the church itself believes) that God is clearly using to give content to the three-thousand-year-old word "Israel" in ever new and fuller ways.

III. The Nature of Israel

We are now led to ask ourselves whether there is any connection between Israel as a nation among the nations and Israel as the People of God. We have said that the usual word for the "people" of Israel which the prophets employ is *'am,* whereas the word for the other nations of the earth is normally *goy*. In fact, when the prophets seek to show how far Israel may have wandered from her true calling as the People of God, they even go so far as to declare that she (i.e., the bride of God) is in reality *lo' 'ammi,* "not my people" (cf. Hosea 1:9). For it is her election that makes her God's *'am,* and not anything native to herself (see above at II); accordingly therefore, if she repudiates her election, as of course she has the power and the free will to do, she chooses to be a mere *goy* (Isa. 1:4) or a heathen people and no longer to be God's special *'am*. Yet, of course, as we have seen, Israel was a *goy* in the first place, or an *ethnos,* as the word is usually rendered when translated into Greek. *Laos,* we should note, usually translated the word *'am*. For Israel, the Children of Abraham, was, in the first place, a natural human unit.

The phrase "The first Jew was a Babylonian" sounds like an interesting paradox. Yet Abraham was never a "Jew." He was, in fact, a Gentile, but one whose *faith* separated him from all other Gentiles of the ancient world. Again, Jacob and Esau were both sons of Isaac, so that, as the ancient Semitic world would suppose, both should have inherited the promises of God. But Esau did not, in fact, appreciate his calling as a son of the promise. What distinguishes Jacob from Esau, therefore, is not Jacob's morality or "goodness," for in many respects Jacob was a repulsive man. The distinguishing factor was that Jacob allowed God to destroy his old ego, so to speak, and to make him into the kind of man that God could use. The name "Israel," therefore, describes the result of a change of heart in one of the two "representative Israelites" of the third generation, and does not here refer to blood or genes. Later again, we read that "a mixed multitude also went up with them" (Ex. 12:38) when Israel came out of Egypt. We should note that there is no suggestion in the book of Exodus that God did not include in the covenant he made at Sinai with "Israel" those pagan Gentiles mentioned here. Again, in his *A History of Israel* (Oxford University Press, Inc., 1932), Vol. 1, pp. 169–170, Theodore H. Robinson opines that the whole tribe of Judah was not originally Israelite by blood. And certainly, throughout the historical period of preexilic Israel, the various elements of the population that the Old Testament calls generically "the Canaanites" were always living alongside of Israel (cf. Judg., ch. 1) in the same towns and villages as Israel, and so were surely continually intermarrying with "the People of God."

Ezekiel, ch. 8, lifts the curtain upon some of the appalling pagan cults that were dear to the heart of Israel in the seventh century. These had probably been introduced by "new converts" dwelling in the very homes in which the Israelites visited and with whom they fraternized. Many Idumeans were forced to become Jews in the second century before Christ, and so should certainly not be considered as Jews by race. In New Testament times, moreover, Galilee was so sparsely Jewish by "race" that it was known as "Galilee of the Gentiles"; and very many Jews by faith in that area must actually have been of alien "blood." This situation arose because many of its inhabitants had probably been forced to undergo circumcision at the point of the sword in the years after the Maccabean wars.

Throughout the Biblical period, however, Israel naturally was *organized* first as an amphictyony (a number of independent tribes united only by a common faith) and then as a monarchy. It was only later, after the return from Exile, that Israel was governed by a high priest. But in each case Israel was in reality a theocracy. Ideally speaking, she never acknowledged any king to be her lord except the Lord (I Sam. 8:7). For Israel's earthly king was never regarded first of all as the ruler of a territory, but was primarily considered to be "the Lord's anointed" over "the Lord's people." This was made evident when the king in Jerusalem to the south was held to be the rightful ruler under God even of the scattered sheep of Israel who had been left among the northern hills after the Assyrian occupation (Jer. 23:1–8). In other words, Israel was more nearly an "idea" first, and then only secondly, and because of the pressures of political life, a national entity. This emphasis continued, moreover, after the exile and the return, for when a high priest then succeeded to the office of king, it was quite clear that "Israel" was not a *goy,* but was indeed a believing community, even though largely scattered over Greece and Egypt, Asia Minor and the isles of the sea, and so was living among many another Gentile *ethnos.* Part of the mystery of Israel, then, is that she has always been a *laos,* even when she had to be an *ethnos* too by force of circumstances.

We must now face the anomaly that it was this same *laos* of which we have been thinking, this veritable People of God, that actually never ceased to rebel (the common Hebrew verb *pasha'*) against its calling to be the Servant People of God. In fact, Israel never ceased to kick against the covenant fellowship and relationship that God had imposed upon his people, when in the beginning he purposed to make them into his light to lighten the Gentiles. Israel's heart, then, was evidently desperately sick, even when it was no more so than is the heart of any of the *goyim* of the earth (see Gen. 6:5; Jer. 17:9; and Jer., ch. 9). Yet it must be admitted that Israel did at times seek to come back to God and ask to be forgiven. And on those occasions God did offer Israel his complete and comprehensive forgiveness. Yet Israel, we read, immediately returned to her old ways and continued in her sin. Something was therefore evidently radically wrong in the relationship between God and Israel—not with God's power to forgive, obviously, but, rather, with Israel's capacity to accept forgiveness. Therefore something radical must necessarily be done to Israel. Forgiveness, it seems, is not enough to bring about the change of heart that God is seeking. Israel's very ego must, in fact, necessarily be destroyed. Such, moreover, is the passionate (the basic meaning of "jealous") covenant love of God, that he is actually willing to take this drastic step in dealing with his beloved bride (see Jer., ch. 7); for he sees that no other way can be effective. This harsh action of God, then, is what Isaiah has called "God's strange work" (Isa. 28:21). But the foolishness of God, Isaiah believes, is wiser than men, and God's thoughts, as Second Isaiah declares (Isa. 55:8), are higher than our thoughts and his ways higher than our ways. In fact, God's covenantal loyalty to Israel is such that he is actually ready to destroy his own beloved, or to "tear her like a lion," as Hosea understands him, if perchance he can thereby smash the hard shell of her heart, and so let the seed contained therein fall into the ground and die (Deut. 32:39). For by no other way can proud Israel become the lowly servant of God's illimitable purpose of love to all nations; for in no other way can she accept God's illimitable and overwhelming forgiveness. That this is not mere theological speculation but is actually historical reality is made clear to us from the pages of the Old Testament itself. For in the year 587 B.C., God did in fact destroy his own covenant people as a national identity and did in fact drive them into the "death" of the Babylonian exile (Ezek. 7:1–2). It was only *thereafter,* moreover, that he brought them forth out of their graves (Ezek., ch. 37), and raised them up to receive from him once again his great forgiveness (Zech. 3:1–5) and the chance to be his *laos,* the veritable people of God, at last.

We can now isolate another aspect of the mystery of Israel, then. For of all the peoples of the earth it is Israel alone whom God has so loved that he chose to deal with her in this extraordinary manner. How tragic it is, then, that Israel did not learn from her own historical experience what it means to be the People of God; for in the years following upon the exile she did not even seem to recognize that God has singled her out when he chose her alone to be the object of his "strange work" of judgment.

Now, even before the days of Second Isaiah's penetrating interpretation of the covenant relationship, the prophet Jeremiah had become aware that the covenant, as it stood, was bound to be ineffective. Israel, the People of God, was in fact too sinful, too rebellious, and too egotistical ever to be able to implement God's forgiveness of her rebellious ways, so as to "go out into the highways and hedges" and compel the nations to come in (cf. Luke 14:15–24), that those nations might share in her feast of good things. It was not the faithfulness of God that was at fault, Jeremiah saw; rather it was the hardness of Israel's heart. Thus we read in Jer. 31:31–33 what he believed God would eventually bring to pass, if God was indeed to be true to the covenant love he had now revealed. Let us then list the salient points of Jeremiah's declaration:

a. The event is still to come.

b. When it does come, it will be God who will act, not man; for God alone can alter the present situation of stalemate.

c. God will then make a new covenant. This will not be an unusual thing for God to do, for it is as the covenant-making God that the Bible portrays him.

d. This covenant is to be with Israel, the *laos* of God, and not with any Gentile nation.

e. It is not to be the kind of covenant that Israel has already known, and that man is free to break.

f. It is to be made with an Israel which will be living in such a relationship to God that each member thereof will want to keep the covenant *sua sponte,* gladly and freely, as the natural outcome of his fellowship with God.

g. This new natural relationship to God will mark the flowering of the perfect "marriage" love; for the bride will then gladly and willingly "keep the law" that her divine husband gave to her as his gift long centuries before, for now she will be wholly committed to her husband in love.

h. This new relationship implies not just a *word* of forgiveness, but also a decisive *act* on God's part. For only when God acts in such a way will Israel be enabled to refrain from wandering away from home; and only then will she really "know the Lord," even as a wife really knows the husband who has made her the queen of his home.

IV. The Mystery of the New Testament's Claim

That claim is this—that it is Jesus who is the fulfillment of the promises of the Old Testament. Consequently, the New Testament declares:

a. It was God who acted, and not man, in the life, death, and resurrection of Jesus.

b. It was God, in Christ, who made the new covenant that Jeremiah had looked for.

c. This covenant is undoubtedly made with Israel, and not with the nations of the earth; that is, it is made with that people which is still the People of God, that *laos* which God called from the beginning to be his servant and instrument for the redemption of the world.

d. By transforming the human heart, God in Christ has actually brought about the new relationship within the covenant of which Jeremiah spoke; for "the new man in Christ" now "knows the Lord" in a new and transforming manner, and so is enabled to "keep the law" in his heart without making any self-conscious effort to do so.

e. The new relationship has, in fact, been effected by an act of God, through his action in Christ of redemptive forgiveness by means of the cross and the resurrection.

The New Testament now goes on to declare that God has done all this in Christ, *within Israel,* in that Jesus himself *is* Israel. According to the flesh, as *ethnos,* Jesus is clearly Israel, for he is born of the line of David. But he is also Israel as *laos* too. We recall how Pilate placed over Jesus' head the superscription "The King of the Jews." Little did Pilate realize that by so doing he was really witnessing to a truth of eternity. In ancient times, men thought of their king as summing up in himself the whole significance of his nation. He was, in fact, in himself the epitome, the representation, the meaning, of his whole subject nation. In this light, then, the early church conspicuously believed, as we can read for ourselves, that the election of all Israel actually found its "end," or its complete fulfillment, and so its *raison d'être,* in this Jesus whom men now called the Christ (see Chapter 4).

Jesus then had come to the Jew first, *prōton,* as he himself repeatedly declared (cf. Mark 7:27; 13:10; Acts 3:26; Rom. 1:16; 2:9–10). The whole New Testament, in fact, believes that Jesus is the fulfillment of the *election of Israel,* for he is indeed the firstborn Son of God (Ex. 4:22). So it is not just that Jesus is "representative" Israel, but also conversely, that Israel, as the elect People of God from of old, now finds her meaning and the "end" of her own election in him. What it means to be called of God and what it means to share in the task of being a light to the Gentiles now leaves the sphere of word and promise, and enters the sphere of fulfillment and event. Again, God now means to continue into the future the task and calling of Israel, in Christ, even until the *plērōma,* the totality of the Gentiles, finally comes in (Rom. 11:25). This "incoming" can and shall take place only because Christ is already the *plērōma* himself, the totality of the Word of God made flesh; for from him there flows the whole fullness of divine grace and truth (John 1:14, 16). "In him all the fullness of God was pleased to dwell" (Col. 1:19); "in him the whole fullness of deity dwells bodily" (Col. 2:9). So, too, it was in the fullness of time that God sent him to be born of a woman (Gal. 4:4). Yet here we meet with a paradox, for Paul can also say, "The church, which is his body, the fullness of him who fills all in all" (Eph. 1:22–23). The church is thus for Paul evidently the actual physical sphere of this fullness of God which is now made known in Christ! Yet the church is still *only* the sphere, the locus, the body, of the *plērōma,* for it is always Christ himself who is the fullness of all things. That, then, is how Paul can bring even the law into this area of revelation. For he speaks of the new revelation of the fullness of love that has happened in Christ, and so can declare consequently that love is the *plērōma* even of the law (Rom. 13:10).

V. The New Testament's Resolution of the "Mystery"

The paradox we have just indicated is exposed in a startling manner, however, when we notice how the New Testament connects the fullness of Christ with the unbelief of Israel. To begin with, we are to remember that the word "Israel" has no plural. Consequently, we are to be clear that the New Testament never speaks in terms of two Israels, as some theologians today seem to take for granted. "The Jews" in the New Testament are not the "old Israel," while "the church" has become the "New Israel." Such language is quite unbiblical. Had not Jeremiah proclaimed that God would make a new covenant *with the house of Israel?* Jeremiah did not say "with a new Israel." For he knew God to be the faithful God; he knew that if God enters into covenant with the people of his choice, then he will never let that people go. Consequently, if that people, because of the hardness of their hearts, cannot recognize that God has now acted in Christ to fulfill their election, and so to enable them, in Christ, to be the sphere, the locus, the body, of Christ's redemptive purpose for the world, then it does not mean that the ancient purpose and plan of God are now frustrated. For if Christ is indeed the *plērōma,* the fullness of *all* things in heaven and earth, then he is also the fullness of Israel's *unbelief* just as truly as he is the fullness of Israel's faith. The point is this, that it is not just when men cooperate with God that his purpose advances; for God can equally well employ men's noncooperation and even rebellion as instruments of his loving purpose. Or, to express this truth in other terms, Jesus the Christ is not only the man, Jesus of Nazareth. For "the Christ," the Greek word for the Hebrew term "the Messiah," is no less than Jesus even as he completes the historical task that Israel failed to perform. That is to say, we only begin to understand the Messiahship of Jesus when we recognize that he includes within himself the history of God's dealings with Israel since the days of Abraham. That, then, is how God is even now using the unbelief of Israel, Paul declares, just as easily as he would have used their faith. What is more, it is actually because of their unbelief that a good thing has indeed come to pass, for the gospel has now gone forth beyond them, and has spread out into the whole world of the *goyim,* the Gentiles (Rom. 11:11).

To express the above ideas in other words, then, we may say that the New Testament offers not the slightest suggestion that "the Jews" are no longer Israel, far less that "the Jews" are damned because, as a whole, they have not believed in Christ as the meaning of their life. For are they not still that same people for whom Christ prayed on the cross: "Father, forgive them; for they know not what they do"? What the New Testament does say is this, however, that, as the Gentiles come in their turn to believe in Christ and to commit their whole lives to him, they are then *added* each day to the one Israel that has been the People of God from the beginning (Acts 2:47; cf. Isa. 44:5); or, to use Paul's vivid metaphor from horticulture, Gentile believers are now *grafted* into the parent stock that is the original Israel, the original *'am* whom the faithful God has certainly never rejected (Rom. 11:17). Some of the branches of that living plant have indeed been broken off (v. 19). For a Jew, like any man, is free to reject his heritage, and to turn his back upon the God of his salvation. But the *whole* olive (v. 17), or the *whole* vine (for this is the commoner metaphor in both Testaments), represents the *wholeness,* the fullness of Israel, that is to say, both Jews and Gentiles together. For they both share now in the fullness, the *plērōma,* of the Godhead that has flowed to us in Christ. That, then, is why there is now neither Jew nor

Gentile, for all share in the new manhood and fullness of Christ.

Yet the mystery still remains that within the wholeness of the one Israel a part of that whole continues to reject the significance of the *plērōma* and has continued to misunderstand what it means to be the *prōton,* the first, in God's scheme for the redemption of the world. Yet, as we have seen, that rejection has not prevented the living God from furthering his purpose of redemption in Christ; in fact, God has actually used to his own glory "Israel's" unbelief, in that he has allowed the Gentiles to be "added in" to "Israel." But Jewish unbelief must also mean that the fullness cannot yet be fullness, except in a proleptic sense. For Christians will never properly understand who the Messiah of the Bible really is until the ancient People of God shall tell them. For the story of God's dealings with Israel in the Old Testament is ultimately to be understood in terms of Christology, for in the unfolding of the tale we witness a divine activity that finds its fulfillment only in Jesus of Nazareth. This reality, therefore, only the "original stock" will ever be able fully to understand, for they understand it from within; the grafted branch, on the other hand, can understand it, and realize its significance only with the help of the Jew. This means that the church can never really be the church as God has willed it to be until the schism that cuts Israel in two is healed. Furthermore, those Gentile sects within the church which have come into being through a peculiar emphasis derived from a particular understanding of Christianity as the faith of the New Testament, without making any effort to estimate this special understanding of theirs in the light of the significance of Israel in the Old Testament—these have lost contact with the root of God's purpose for the world, which is to be obtained through the unity of his one and only People of God. On the other hand, however, the fullness about which we have been thinking has actually been revealed to us as *agapē,* or love; and so the fullness that is revealed to us in Christ is actually not "fullness" at all, but is, rather, to be understood as "emptiness"! For Christ's *agapē* is no less than a complete self-emptying, a pouring out of itself, in order that the other might share in the wholeness and the joy of the *plērōma.* (Isa. 53:10–11; Phil. 2:1–11.) Such an all-embracing "emptiness," therefore, can surely embrace both those who believe and those who do not.

The one Israel, then, as the Christian sees the issue, is compounded of two elements: those who believe in Christ and those who do not yet believe. Paul does not, of course, infer that the line between the two is a straight Jew-Gentile line; for many a baptized Gentile, now that he is a member of Israel, loses his vision of his calling, and steps aside from the race; and many an unbaptized Jew just as surely sees that the basic law of the whole universe is, in fact, that "death and resurrection" motif which is to be found throughout the whole of the Old Testament, that is, the book of Israel. Both elements are to be found in Israel, then, just as in the days of the patriarchs, in fact, ever since the beginning of the election of Israel. For Abraham's unbelieving nephew Lot also went along with his believing uncle to the Land of Promise, and Abraham accepted him as a member of the chosen community even when Lot decided to dally in Sodom. Evidently it is not for man to say who is of the elect of God and who is not, for God alone is Judge. Isaac again had two sons, Esau and Jacob, and both of these lads entered into the promises made to their grandfather Abraham. The one was clearly consciously aware of his calling; the other evidently was not. The one was therefore "chosen," whereas the other God "chose" not to use. Yet Jacob was chosen, not to be saved, but to serve in love that unbelieving brother of his, with the end and purpose in view that Esau might be saved from his state of rebellion! So, then, is "Jacob" ever truly saved himself until "Esau" too finds salvation? Is the church ever really the "saved" People of God until the Jews too find salvation? Will Jews and Gentiles together form his body, since only then will *all* men finally be saved? (Rom. 11:12; Isa. 45:23.) This is no mere academic question, for as we began by recalling, Jews and Christians are living together as neighbors in the same street.

The view of the New Testament, then, is that "the Jews" are in fact one body with "the Christians," for both together are the one Israel, the one People of God. Yet the mystery remains that "the Jews" still do not believe that to be part of that body is to share in what is really a gift of grace, and of grace alone. For "the Jews" have not yet seen in Christ that man cannot earn membership in the body either by keeping the law, or by offering to God a noble and virtuous life. That is to say, "the Jews" have never grasped the principle which Hosea, Jeremiah, and Second Isaiah so deeply understood, that at the very heart of the living God himself there stands a cross.

The mystery of the Jews, then, rests ultimately in the simple fact that they are still here. The Jews are still that People of God which was prepared over the centuries by God (Isa. 49:1–3; 50:4–9) to be the body that God proposed to use when the fullness of time should come (Heb. 10:5–7). Yet, when it came, that body met with crucifixion and death. "The Jews," however, have not yet entered into the secret of the crucifixion for themselves; and they still suppose that what God requires of them is, basically, to lead a virtuous life. Now, a vital aim of the law of Moses was to offer Israel a new and holy way of life. Moreover, that perfect, whole, complete (cf. *plērōma*) form of society under God, that is legislated for in the Torah, might well be summarized by the Old Testament word *shalom*. Let us be clear that the word means much more than does the modern English word "peace." For it describes men and women living in perfect harmony with themselves and with each other, as together they live in harmony with God. Moreover, the cement of this *shalom*, so to speak, is what the noun *tsedaqah* represents. This latter word, again, can mean much more than the English word "righteousness" conveys. Dare a Christian suggest that it was the error of main line Judaism, after the regulating influence of Ezra had made itself felt, to define this noun in terms of good works and almsgiving? (See Chapter 7.) But the Isaiah of the exile, a century before Ezra appeared on the scene, had already described a situation with a wholly new dimensional content, and had already used the word *tsedaqah* to describe it. For him, the word meant no less than loving, saving, outgoing, creative activity. This means that his picture of the Suffering Servant in Isa., ch. 53, is virtually a picture of this word as it is meant to "become flesh" in the life of Israel. And there *tsedaqah* is certainly not mere goodness. Isaiah, ch. 53, instead describes the very negation of the self of the Servant in order that the Gentile world might be saved.

"The Jews" have suffered indeed, suffered as no nation has ever done for so long a period or so intensively. And yet many American Jews today possess no clue whatsoever to this monstrous suffering (see Henry Cohen, "The Idea of God in Jewish Education," *Judaism,* Vol. 12, No. 2, pp. 165 ff.), and cannot build a theodicy for themselves into which suffering can be anywhere fitted. But did not Jesus say: "He who does not gather with me scatters" (Matt. 12:30)? Jewish suffering has therefore never become the "cement" of God's *shalom* for the world that it was meant to be in the providence of God.

Humbly, then, we would suggest that it is this most significant element in the whole of the Old Testament revelation, viz., the redemptive suffering that God himself knows in his own heart and experience, that "the Jews" have failed to understand, and consequently have failed to connect with their calling as the People of God. Ezra's successors have therefore continued to regard the cross of Christ as an incomprehensible conundrum. And yet it was a Jew, for the writer of the Fourth Gospel was a member of the Old Testament People of God, who fully appreciated what Jesus meant in declaring: "My *shalom* I give to you" (John 14:27); for John was completely and existentially aware that Jesus was giving to the whole of Israel, to the whole People of God, the *plērōma* of which he spoke; for he believed that Jesus himself *was* the *plērōma,* which, as the very Word of God, became flesh and dwelt among us, only to be crucified for us and by us, and for and by the whole world of men.

The Christian, in sincere dialogue, would thus suggest that since "the Jews" do not know what it means to be crucified with Christ, they cannot know what it means to be raised with Christ, to be raised into that *plērōma,* that fullness of life which death is not able to touch. For the latter is Christ's gift to those who accept his calling to watch with him one hour at Gethsemane (Rom. 6:1–11; Matt. 10:38–39).

Israel, then, is one indeed, but the mystery of Israel is this, that it is one in the sense that Siamese twins are one. Only, in this case, one of the twins that makes up the one body, which is in reality the body of Christ, has accepted in humility and boundless gratitude all that God, in his grace, has done to include him in the completion, the perfection, the wholeness, the *plērōma* of all things. The other twin has not, for he believes that, as Israel, unlike the Gentiles, he is already living in the presence of God.

Chapter Three

THE MEANING OF PROPHECY

Jews and Christians share the Old Testament. Moses, Samuel, Isaiah, and Jeremiah, and all the great company of the prophets, are our common heritage. In the area of the academic study of the prophets, Jewish and Christian scholars work side by side, sometimes criticizing each other's work, often corroborating each other's research. Unfortunately, the ordinary churchman and synagogue worshiper have scarcely heard of this heartfelt cooperation among Biblical scholars. C. J. de Catanzaro, Professor at Seabury-Western Theological Seminary, Evanston, Illinois, seeks to express here, for the average reader and from the Christian point of view, what many decades of scholarship have led us to understand about the significance of the prophets.

—*The Editor*

The Nicene Creed, the most ancient and authoritative confession of the Christian faith, asserts that the Holy Spirit "spake by [i.e., through] the prophets." It thus affirms the role of the Old Testament, and particularly of the prophetic writings, as a vehicle of the revelation of God. Our concern here is to discover what they have to say about the Israel of today.

In a sense, the whole of the Old Testament is prophetic Scripture. Not only does the heading "the Prophets" (*nebi'im*) in the Hebrew canon of Scripture include considerably more than our conventional prophetic books, namely, the historical writing of Joshua, Judges, Samuel, and Kings, which it labels "the Former Prophets," as distinct from the others (minus Daniel and Lamentations), which it labels "the Latter Prophets;" no part of the Old Testament is wholly uninfluenced by the prophetic spirit. Thus in the Pentateuch itself, Moses is regarded as the prototype of prophecy (see Deut. 18:15, 18). In the New Testament not only the Prophets proper and the Pentateuch but other writings, particularly the Psalter, are cited as prophetic (see, e.g., Mark 12:35–37; Acts 2:30).

In this wider sense, therefore, prophecy represents that Biblical heritage that is common to Christianity and Judaism. For Christians of all kinds, prophecy is thus the main line of the *praeparatio evangelica.* Granting this thesis, however, Christians have differed greatly in their approach to prophecy, and still continue to do so. The aim of this chapter, therefore, will be that of assessing some of these differences, and of clearing aside certain difficulties and misunderstandings that continue to beset Christians and Jews alike.

I. Prophecy in the Old Testament

Prophecy has a long history in the Old Testament. The very terminology itself displays some variety. In the older literature we find such varied terms as "man of God" (*'ish-ha-Elohim,* I Sam. 9:6; II Kings 1:9), and "seer" (*ḥozeh,* II Sam. 24:11; Amos 7:12; *ro'eh,* I Sam. 9:11). Later, the term "prophet" (*nabi'*) becomes universal; its use may fairly justify the rendering of the noun as "spokesman," usually of God, but in one significant passage (Ex. 7:1; cf. ch. 4:16), of man.

At an early date, however, a different type of prophet appears. Sometimes he is closely associated with the "sons of the prophets" (e.g., II Kings 4:38 ff.); at other times he disclaims such association (e.g., Amos 7:14), though his distinctiveness is not always apparent to his contemporaries or even to the prophet himself. Despite all external resemblances, however, this type of prophet stands out increasingly as the champion of the covenant of the Lord and its implications of loyalty and obedience.

The rise of these prophets was the result of the constant tension in Israel's life between the divine election and God's demands, on the one hand, and the tendency for Israel "to become like the nations" (Ezek. 20:32), on the other. Materially and culturally, some degree of assimilation was clearly necessary because of Israel's settlement in the Land of the Canaanites. But it was accompanied by the tendency to assimilate religiously as well, if not by the conscious discarding of the religious tradition, at least by distorting or submerging it. The prophets were thus conservatives, recalling Israel to the national faith, to a worship of the Lord that could brook no rivals, whether the Baals of Canaan and their constantly recrudescent fertility rites or foreign gods imported through contacts with neighboring peoples. As against the religious and ethical laxity that was corroding Israel's social and political life, they affirmed the sacred traditions of Israel's past.

In this, however, they were no mere archaizers. Not only did they treat the Mosaic faith and its ethical implications as supremely relevant for the present, they applied it in new and sometimes startling ways. Thus they bade Israel learn that God would execute his judgment not merely on their enemies, but on his own people as well for their disloyalty and disobedience, indeed, that he would use the very enemies of Israel as his instruments of punishment. In varying ways this is proclaimed by the preexilic prophets such as Amos, Hosea, Micah, and Isaiah. Isaiah thus described Assyria as the rod of God's anger (Isa. 10:5), useful indeed for chastising his people, yet due to be discarded when its purpose had been fulfilled, and to be humbled for its overweening pride (Isa. 10:12–15). In much the same terms, Jeremiah spoke of God's using the Chaldeans and Nebuchadnezzar for his purpose (Jer., ch. 27). With this emphasis on the moral nature of God went the gradual unfolding of that monotheism which was implicit in the exclusiveness of the Mosaic faith (see Ex. 34:14), but which had to wait for its full and explicit statement for the great prophet of the return, the so-called Second Isaiah (see Isa. 44:6; 45:5–6).

II. The Prophets in History

It is clear that the activity and the message of the prophets has its setting in Israel's history. The word of the Lord "comes" to the prophet, not in a timeless vacuum, but in the context of that concrete situation in which the people of God find themselves, at that time and in that place. The prophet speaks on God's behalf, therefore, not in terms of abstract principles, but in terms of that situation, and with relevance to it.

Special caution is needed in dealing with the predictive element of prophecy. Its existence cannot be ignored or lightly passed over. Thus true prediction is recognized as a criterion of true prophecy (e.g., Deut. 18:22; Jer. 28:16–17), though not the only one. The same context in Deuteronomy, and other passages elsewhere (e.g., Lev. 20:6, 27), condemn all forms of soothsaying and divination. The prophets were, of course, deeply concerned with the future of Israel. Although they spoke on God's behalf in the concrete situation, their message transcended the immediate present, and was relevant to the wider context of God's plans and purposes for Israel. With their particular "psychic" personalities, the prophets often had a specially vivid awareness of that future of which they were conscious because of their insight into God's dealings with his people. Thus Amos could "see" the fate of Amaziah, the priest of Bethel, in the context of the coming Assyrian invasion (Amos 7:16–17), and Isaiah vividly describes the relentless advance of Sennacherib's armies on Jerusalem (Isa. 10:27–32). Similarly, the coming restoration of Israel was so vivid and vital a fact to the Second Isaiah, that he would strain poetic imagery to the limit to depict the wondrous change about to take place.

Accordingly, the predictions of the prophets must themselves be seen in the context of Israel's history. That history records notable instances of the fulfillment of prophetic prediction. Thus that doom which the preexilic prophets foresaw with increasing vividness actually came upon the Northern Kingdom with its destruction at the hands of Sargon II in 721 B.C., and on the Southern Kingdom and the Davidic dynasty with the fall of Jerusalem in 586. Then, as the Second Isaiah had recognized, the triumph of Persia meant the restoration of Judah and Jerusalem, and the exiles began to drift back after 538 B.C. Thus the main pattern of the fulfillment was achieved.

It must, however, be admitted that the fulfillment was not always literal. Thus the triumph of Persia was not, immediately, accompanied by that humiliation of Babylon which the Second Isaiah had envisaged (Isa. 47:1–9), nor by any mass return of the exiles to Jerusalem, let alone the fulfillment of Israel's role of mediating the knowledge of God to the nations. In the prophetic perspective, there is a certain foreshortening of the future, and understandably so. Furthermore, the prophets are not the privileged exponents of a deterministic plan to which God is mechanically bound. On the contrary, Scripture affirms the sovereignty of God, and consequently his freedom to adapt and change his plans. Every prophecy thus contains, implicitly or explicitly, the condition—

> If you are willing and obedient,
> you shall eat the good of the land;
> but if you refuse and rebel,
> you shall be devoured.
> (Isa. 1:19–20.)

It is thus possible for God to "repent," and to change his plan, according as men respond to his will, or to refuse to do so. "Did he [Hezekiah] not fear the Lord and entreat the favor of the Lord, and did not the Lord repent of the evil which he had pronounced against them?" (Jer. 26:19.)

Apocalyptic prediction follows the same pattern in this respect. It is futile, as some earnest Christians have done, to look in the pages of The Book of Daniel for detailed information about the careers of modern totalitarian dictators. The apparent "predictions" of which that book is full are, for the most part, the history of the preceding centuries rewritten in symbolic form, the author having projected himself back into the past. His particular concern is with the anti-Jewish measures of Antiochus Epiphanes, who ruled Syria from 175 until 163 B.C., and desecrated the Temple in 167 B.C. When he looks toward the immediate future, his descriptions become vaguer. Here, too, we find a prediction that was fulfilled. The tyrant indeed came "to his end, with none to help him" (Dan. 11:45) within a couple of years of the writing of the book, though the actual circumstances of the fulfillment did not coincide with the author's expectations with anything like literal exactitude.

III. Prophecy and the New Testament

The New Testament is built on the cornerstone of the proclamation that in the person of Jesus of Nazareth, the Messiah has come, and that in him "all the promises of God are 'Yea' " (II Cor. 1:20). In him all the Messianic promises of the Old Testament are more than fulfilled, but not in a rigidly literal manner. Although accepting the confession of his Messiahship, our Lord refused to conform to the popular image of the Messianic king, even though it could claim support from the letter of prophecy. Instead, he stressed other patterns, such as that of the heavenly Son of Man (see Mark 14:62) and that of the Suffering Servant (ch. 10:45). Small wonder that the New Testament writers, in their search for Old Testament pointers to the life and person of Christ, should have pressed even apparently irrelevant texts into service as testimonia (cf. Matt. 2:23; John 19:24).

Likewise, the New Testament sees the spiritual destiny of Israel as being fulfilled in the Israel "according to the Spirit," the church, those who share Abraham's faith in God and have become his offspring through incorporation into Christ (cf.

Gal. 3:29). It should be noted that the Old Testament always links the Messianic expectation with the fulfillment of Israel's destiny. So in Christ, who is seen as the "light to lighten the Gentiles" (Luke 2:32; cf. Isa. 49:6), the destiny of Israel and of Jerusalem is being fulfilled. It is thus entirely in accord with the New Testament to view the prophetic vision that

> out of Zion shall go forth instruction,
> and the word of the Lord from Jerusalem
> (Isa. 2:3)

as having been fulfilled in the Pentecostal outpouring of the Holy Spirit and the apostolic mission of the church into all the world, not only to the Jews of the Dispersion, but also to the Gentiles. The same can be said of the visions of the future glory of Jerusalem contained in the oracles of the latter part of The Book of Isaiah.

It must not, however, be forgotten that the New Testament itself bears witness to an unfulfilled promise of God concerning Israel. Thus Paul in Rom., chs. 9 to 11, speaks of a destiny yet to be fulfilled for the historic Israel "according to the flesh," even though it has not yet obeyed the gospel, as we saw in Chapter 2. "If their rejection means the reconciliation of the world, what will their acceptance mean but life from the dead?" (Rom. 11:15.) Similarly, the language about the future transformation of nature, so common in Isa., chs. 40 to 66, while in its immediate context it may be treated as a poetic hyperbole of God's sweeping aside of all obstacles to the fulfillment of his plan for the restoration of his people, is taken up anew in an eschatological context; we may note here particularly the language of the Third Isaiah about "new heavens and a new earth" (Isa. 65:17; II Peter 3:13; Rev. 21:1), and in the same way his language about the new Jerusalem (Isa., ch. 60; Rev., ch. 21).

The true understanding of Scripture thus precludes any use of prophecy analogous to divination, to prognosticate the future of individuals and nations. The attempt, so common in the church's history, to identify persons and events in our own times as literal fulfillment of Scriptural prediction is not only doomed to failure, disappointment, and frustration, but it is repugnant to that very Word of God which Scripture enshrines in human language. Rather, the attentive use of prophecy enables us to discern in the events of Israel's history the exemplar of God's continued activity and involvement in the world of man, his constant demand that his people render him wholehearted obedience. In other words, it is the whole of the Old Testament, and of the story of the People of God to be found therein, that is "prophetic" in the Biblical sense of the word. For the whole Old Testament is a forward-looking book, and bears within the history it records the promise of the coming of the Word as human flesh, and of that ultimate fulfillment of all things which Isa., chs. 60 to 66, describes in such majestic language.

IV. The Present Relevance of Old Testament Prophecy

Some Christians, forgetting II Cor. 1:20, have not been satisfied with the New Testament terms of fulfillment, but have looked for a more literal fulfillment of Old Testament prophecy in their own time. For them, as also for the Jews, who have refused to accept this fulfillment, the question of fulfillment is bound to be an acute one.

For the Jews, the Messianic problem has been specially important. There has been no lack of Messianic claimants accepted as such in their times by a great number of Jews, from Simon bar Kosibah (Bar-Cochba) in the second century, not to mention earlier pretenders, to Shabbethai Zebi in the seventeenth, and some even later. Their failure, accompanied in some cases by frightful military disasters and brutal measures of repression, has, understandably, led to the abandonment of any hope of a personal Messiah on the part of many, if not most, Jews in our day.

More recently many Jews, and some Christians as well, have alleged a literal fulfillment of Biblical prophecy in the establishment of the Zionist state in the Holy Land. This has its obvious difficulties. Apart from the political circumstances of the genesis of this state, it cannot be ignored that Zionism, up to the present, has had a predominantly secular aspect. Nor has the return of many Jews to their ancient homeland, while it has provided an obvious escape from that anti-Semitism, overt or latent, which has been the continuing disgrace of the so-called "Christian" lands, been accompanied by any notable revival or renewal of their faith. So far this endeavor of the "Israel according to the flesh," despite many laudable features, instead of enabling it to become a spiritual leaven for mankind, has resulted merely in the establishment and maintenance of one more national state and the rousing of the fierce antagonism of its neighbors.

It is on sound Biblical grounds, then, that certain groups of orthodox Jews have refused the facile identification of the Zionist state and its achievements with the fulfillment of prophecy, and rightly point out the absence of a personal Messiah. The mere fact that some of those achievements bear some external resemblance to that transformation of nature of which the prophets speak (e.g., Isa. 35:1–2) is even less reason for Christians to forget sound principles of Biblical interpretation.

Chapter Four

THE MESSIANIC HOPE

Unwary Christians sometimes entertain the idea that the Old Testament is a collection of Messianic proof texts that point to the Christ of the New Testament, and so they wonder why Jews do not see in those texts what they themselves understand when they read them.

As a matter of fact, Jewish and Christian scholars have worked closely together in recent years in an attempt to understand the essential Messianic significance of the Old Testament as a whole. The subject is therefore central for a volume such as this, and is dealt with in a scholarly manner by Norman K. Gottwald, professor at Andover Newton Theological School. In Professor Gottwald's defense it must be stated that the Editor has reduced the original material by about one third, as he has done to all the contributors to this volume, including even his own chapters!

—The Editor

The Messianic hope is common to Jews and Christians, yet forms an obvious point of difference between them. It is the contention of the Christian faith that the Old Testament hope for a Messiah has been met in Jesus of Nazareth. Judaism objects that it has not. What is at issue in the discussion? Which party is right?

Complicating our survey of the historical material is the confusion of nomenclature in the description of Jewish futurism. Notably vexing are the divergent meanings given to eschatology, apocalypticism, and Messianism itself. Each writer in this field must delimit his terms.

I. The Biblical Period

Eschatology is the widest of the three terms, coextensive with the futuristic belief. From as early as the tenth century B.C., as testified by Gen. 12:1–3; Num. 24:17; Deut. 33:26–29, the intense belief in the blessing of God upon Israel in history was fully operative. Admittedly, the belief only begins to fill out with detailed motifs and to receive prominence with the prophets, so that it may be preferable to say that the preprophetic futurism was protoeschatology. Nonetheless, the inclusive use of the term "eschatology" properly emphasizes the continuum of development from broad, undifferentiated national futurism, through specific prophetic forms of national futurism, to individualistic futurism. This usage is justified by the fact that these three stages do not simply succeed one another but remain side by side in later Judaism and Christianity as, so to speak, different wings on one stage.

Apocalypticism, again, is that form of eschatology which stressed the gulf between the present evil age and the future redeemed age. It is primarily an ethical dualism which secondarily implies the gathering of cosmic forces in the service of good or evil. The whole world, now under the curse of sin, will be renovated or replaced in the future redemption. Apocalyptic forms of eschatology are generally highly colored with the fantastic garb of ancient Near Eastern folklore and mythology. While eschatology is as old as the Davidic empire, apocalypticism is not older than the exile at most, and its fully developed representatives are from the period 165 B.C. to A.D. 100, i.e., Daniel in the Old Testament, Revelation in the New Testament, and several of the Pseudepigrapha to be described below. Apocalypticism, with its doctrine of the two ages, answers the crucial question as to why evil seems rampant and predominant in this age; and in its belief in the resurrection of the righteous (and often the wicked also) it answers to the need for vindication of the righteous and judgment of the wicked in the world to come. Thus it served a pastoral, consolatory purpose.

Messianism is employed loosely, at times, to refer to eschatological expectations of a national character, i.e., excluding the fate of the individual. Wherever the prophets, or even earlier traditionists, speak of a coming era of peace and righteousness for Israel and for the nations, it may accordingly he described as Messianism. But this is a seriously misleading complication of the endeavor to discriminate among the types of futuristic beliefs. It is accurate to speak of Messianism only where an individual redeemer—the Messiah himself—is being pictured. If this is recognized, Messianism appears nowhere in the Palestinian canon, although Messianism-eschatology does. The first occurrence of Messianism is in the intertestamental literature of the Pseudepigrapha, the Dead Sea Scrolls, the New Testament, and the Talmud. How this is to be squared with the occurrence of the Hebrew word for "Messiah" (*mashiaḥ,* "the anointed") in several Old Testament passages has yet to be explained. Furthermore, the significant figures of the Servant of Yahweh (Isa. 42:1–4; 49:1–6; 50:4–9; 52:13 to 53:12) and the Son of Man (Dan., ch. 7), which have a quasi-individual character, must be finally recognized as futuristic and yet distinguishable from the Messiah in a strict sense. They are, in fact, representations of Israel or of some part of Israel. As we shall see, the separation of these "persons" in Judaism and their combination in Christianity has allowed both religions in good faith to use the same terms in markedly different senses.

"Messiah" is the English transliteration of Hebrew *mashiaḥ* and Aramaic *meshiḥa,* a noun meaning "the anointed one." The complete expression is *meshiaḥ Yahweh,* "the one anointed or consecrated of Yahweh." When we take into account that oil was poured or smeared on objects (temples, cultic pillars, weapons) and on persons (kings, priests, prophets) to set them aside for religious functions, i.e, to consecrate or sanctify them to their new roles, it becomes plain that the expression is in fact a metaphor for "the one consecrated of Yahweh" or "the one sanctified of Yahweh."

The noun *mashiaḥ* appears thirty-seven times in the Old Testament. As with the verb, it is largely with reference to the king. In four cases the high priest is called *mashiaḥ* (Lev. 4:3, 5, 16; 6:22; and possibly in Ps. 84:9), and the patriarchs (or possibly Israel) are once called "my anointed ones" (Ps. 105:15=I Chron. 16:22). In Isa. 45:1, the Persian Cyrus is addressed by God as "my anointed." Two messiahs are referred to cryptically in Dan. 9:25–26, but their identity is disputed. They may be respectively the sixth-century priest Joshua and the Maccabean Onias III, *or* they may be political figures such as Cyrus and one of the Seleucid kings. The remaining twenty-seven occurrences of *mashiaḥ* are almost certainly allusions to actual rulers of the United Kingdom of Israel or of the Divided Kingdoms of Judah and Israel.

Unquestionably the roots of Jewish Messianism are intertwined in the soil of the ancient Israelite kingship which lasted from the reign of Saul about 1000 B.C. to the fall of Jerusalem in 586 B.C. and was either fully restored (Hasmonaeans, 134–63, 40–37 B.C.), abortively reestablished (Bar-Cochba, A.D. 132–135), or wistfully longed for (Zerubbabel, ca. 522–518 B.C.). Israelite kingship was a complex political and religious phenomenon. Here we can do no more than examine certain of its aspects that are germane to later Messianism.

1. *The king stood in a unique and enduring filial relation to God.* In II Sam., ch. 7, the religiopolitical program of Israelite kingship is set forth. Yahweh says of David's sons, collectively understood as a dynasty: "I will be his father, and he shall be my son. When he commits iniquity, I will chasten him with the rod of men, with the stripes of the sons of men; but I will not remove my steadfast love from him as I took it from Saul, whom I put away from before you. And your

house and your kingdom shall be made sure forever before me; your throne shall be established forever" (vs. 14–16). In one of the psalms used at the coronation of the king, Yahweh declares:

> I have set my king on Zion, my holy hill.

And the king echoes him:

> I will declare the decree of Yahweh:
> He said to me, "You are my son,
> today I have begotten you."
> (Ps. 2:6–7.)

The sonship of the king was adoptive and subjected him to chastisement by God as required, but it was an intimate relationship not given to other men and it was a relationship extended to all those in the line of David. Here is clearly the origin of the notion of Messiah as "Son of God."

2. *The king was representative of the people to God and of God to the people.* He was protector of the people and spokesman for the community. He bore the brunt of God's wrath against Israel, and, at his best, he led in the reforms and in repentance that reestablished communion between God and the people. From the side of God, the king was "son" or "servant," and from the side of the people he was "shepherd" or "lamp of Israel."

This representative function of the king was an instance of what has been called "corporate personality"—the concept of a social or religious organism as a single personality. The belief is more directly expressed in the quasi-Messianic notion of the Servant and the Son of Man. To be sure, the people of Israel was not conceived as a king per se, but because Israel was conceivable as a single personality, the line of her kings could be so conceived. The connection between the enduring people and the enduring dynasty was close and dramatically indicative of God's nearness to and provision for Israel. The representative significance of the king, which is stronger than symbolism as we rationalistic

Westerners usually conceive it, does not depend upon any particular theory about the role of the king in the cult. That he had a cultic role to play and did so on a larger scale than was once recognized seems clear. He probably represented the people on cultic occasions but whether he also represented God in an annual "enthronement festival" is still a moot point on which there is as yet insufficient evidence.

3. *The king was exemplar of human obedience to God's will.* In his person were to be exhibited wisdom and righteousness par excellence. All those virtues which make for peace and social well-being are to flow first from the ruler. The sealing with oil was merely the sign of an inner charisma that would send forth streams of blessing upon the community. Thus the *locus classicus* of the spirit-infused virtues of the king, Isa. 11:1–9, even with its reference to the stump of the dynasty (v. 1), expressed the preexilic hope that was directed not to some distant or superhuman being but to each newly ascending monarch.

4. *The king's rule is potentially universal.* Since David was the prototype of kings in Israel, his conquest of the greater part of the territory between the Nile and the Euphrates Rivers served as a model of what a righteous king could expect. Whether "universal" is the proper term for describing this aspect of the king's rule is problematic. Apart from their much-debated cultic interpretation, poetic allowance should doubtless be granted to such passages as:

> "Ask of me, and I will make the nations your heritage,
> and the ends of the earth your possession.
> You shall break them with a rod of iron,
> and dash them in pieces like a potter's vessel."
>
> Now therefore, O kings, be wise;
> be warned, O rulers of the earth.
>
> (Ps. 2:8–10.)

Yet there is a well-established hope within the poetic exuberance. Thus the laudatory title "Prince of Peace" (*sar shalom,* Isa. 9:6) refers both to the peace that the king will impose upon Israel and the world by destroying or retributing wrongdoers *and* the peace that fills his own life as the obedient son of Yahweh, the true king of Israel.

As the Israelite monarchy drew toward a close, the belief in the continuation of David's line did not cease. It would be incorrect to say that any text in the Hebrew Old Testament clearly points to the belief in the Messiah as the king of the final age in the later Jewish or Christian senses. Nonetheless, the tension between expected righteous kings and actual evil kings experienced in preexilic times was supplemented in the exilic age by the tension between the promise of an enduring Davidic dynasty and the actual failure of the Davidic lineage to possess political power. This tension had the effect of underlining the futuristic element in the view of kingship. In other words, religiohistorical tensions and crises brought the incipient Messianism of Israelite kingship farther into the mainstream of eschatology. A Davidic ruler was not on the throne of Judah *now,* but in the near future he would be. Haggai and Zechariah actually identified Zerubbabel as the new king whom they called "branch" and "signet of Yahweh," terms that are complements to the preexilic designation of the legitimate king as "anointed."

The Suffering Servant of Isaiah of the exile is a personification of the collective Israel. Although he bears some royal traits, the Servant image points clearly to the normative vocation of Israel. It is a broadly eschatological conception but it has no direct ties with the views of kingship in Israel. In fact, the same prophet who limned the Servant portrait also transferred the religiopolitical title of Messiah to Cyrus the Persian king (Isa. 45:1)! In a somewhat analogous manner, the Son of Man in Daniel represents the collective "saints of the Most High." The Son of Man has more definite royal traits than the Servant figure, since he is a counterpart to, and an actual replacement for, the evil kingdoms of this world previously described by the apocalyptist. Yet the Son of Man receives his status and power from beyond history, since he comes "on the clouds" and his coming breaks history decisively. Whereas the Servant was to work within the structure of a world empire, the Son of Man brings the era of world empires to an end. Interestingly, however, in the apocalyptic book of Daniel no connection is drawn between individual and collective eschatology. The resurrection of the dead in ch. 12 stands unassimilated with the idea of the Son of Man = saints of the Most High. For the Biblical period, therefore, we must conclude that the later fully developed belief in a Messiah, i.e., Messianism proper, is absent.

II. The Intertestamental Period

It was the intertestamental period that witnessed the genuine flowering of Messianism as an articulate expectation of a ruler of the final age. In other words, Messianism arises where an end to history is definitely expected and where an Israelite king is to serve either as the ruler in the world to come or, more frequently, as the ruler in a transitional (chiliastic or millennïal) age that leads from world history as previously known to the world to come.

There can be no mistaking the fact that the catastrophic wars of the Jews with the Seleucids and Romans, and the civil disturbances and religious controversies among sects and parties of Jews in the three centuries from 168 B.C. to A.D. 135 can best explain the remarkable burgeoning of Messianic hopes in close association with the eschatological ideas that frequently took on the sharp dualistic forms and brilliant images of apocalypticism. Often the mythical garb of the primal age is employed to describe the condition of the end time, with the result that Enoch, Lamech, Noah, and others from Genesis appear as heroes in the intertestamental literature. It was even possible to equate the Son of Man = Elect One = Messiah with the venerable Enoch who, formerly taken into heaven (Gen. 5:24), will return as God's agent at the end of history (I Enoch, chs. 46 to 48; 62 to 71).

Among the exemplars of the Messianic hope in the intertestamental literature are the Pseudepigrapha: the Ethiopic Book of Enoch (I Enoch), especially Parables of the Similitudes (chs. 37 to 71); The Testaments of the Twelve Patriarchs; The Psalms of Solomon, notably chs. 17 to 18; The Syriac Apocalypse of Baruch; and Fourth Ezra. To these should also be added relevant passages from the Dead Sea Scrolls, such as The Manual of Discipline (1QS 9:11), the Damascus Document (CDC 7:20–21; 20:14), The Rule of the Congregation (II. 11–22), and The Blessings (V. 20–29).

A wealth of motifs in the Messianic age crops up in this literature, forming what Klausner calls "the Messianic chain": signs of the nearness of the Messiah's coming, the tribulation of the saints, the forerunner Elijah, the trumpet of deliverance, the ingathering of the exiles, the conversion of proselytes, the war with Gog and Magog, the millennial rule of the Messiah, the renovation of the world, the Day of Judgment, the resurrection of the dead, and the world to come or eternal life.

First, it is noteworthy in this development that individual and collective eschatological motifs are brought together in a sequence, so that Israel's historical redemption and the resurrection of the individual Israelite become stages in the same drama. An apocalyptic spirit pervades the whole, since the rule of the Messiah generally culminates in the passing away of this wicked age and the coming of the new age of God's righteousness. Particularly striking is the way in which a heaven-originated, angelic-like being, a sort of prototypal or archetypal man who is the agent of God's final deliverances, is brought into connection with the continuing mundane figure of a kingly historical redeemer. The two conceptions were not systematized, and it is evident that this simultaneous interpenetration and incongruity appears in the early Christian views as well as in several of the Jewish Pseudepigrapha, although not in the Qumran sect, so far as we can presently judge.

Secondly, however, it should be stressed that "the Messianic chain" was extremely variable in content and order. No two descriptions are identical; links are omitted or rearranged and the nuances are richly varied through the free and often chaotic use of colorful images. The ingredients of the Messianic motifs always retained plasticity in Judaism but the fluid state of the motifs in the intertestamental period contrasts with their greater fixity after A.D. 135 and shows both the ideological flexibility of Judaism in this period and also the several tentative lines along which notions were being developed in a climate of vigorous sectarian debate and historical tumult.

The disastrous wars with Rome in A.D. 66–70 and 132–135, spearheaded by Zealots who thought they could precipitate the Kingdom of God on earth, shaped the Messianic hope in significant ways. The destruction of Jerusalem in A.D. 70 stimulated the political side of the Messianic hope, which led some sixty years later to the endorsement by most of the Jewish religious leadership of the military insurrectionist Bar-Cochba as Messiah. The failure of Bar-Cochba's revolt against Rome diminished the political element of Messianism, or rather, projected it into the future. It particularly aroused official disapproval of attempts that were continually made in Judaism to calculate the time of the Messiah's coming or to identify the Messiah with some contemporary man. The miraculous aspects of Messiah were heightened in subsequent centuries, especially as the main centers of Jewish life shifted from the Palestinian homeland to Babylon and later to Europe.

Throughout later Judaism, suffering enters significantly into the Messianic portraiture but not in the direct sense that the Messiah himself suffers redemptively. There is no suggestion that Messiah ben Joseph's death was to be atoning, even in the sense that the death of Maccabean martyrs was regarded by some as vicariously atoning (IV Macc. 6:29; 17:21 ff.). On the other hand, the suffering of Israel and her repentant response to God's discipline was thought to have preparatory value for the last days and was even regarded by some as hastening the coming of the Messiah. The so-called "birth pangs of Messiah" were never the suffering of the Messiah proper but rather the suffering of the age that would give birth to the Messiah. At first it seems curious that Judaism, which experienced suffering so acutely and deduced religious and moral lessons from it, failed to see any role for a suffering Messiah. This may be partially explained by a reaction against Christianity, but largely it is accounted for by the limitation and specialization of the Messianic hope. Suffering and sorrow belong to eschatology in the wider sense, whereas the Messiah himself always belongs to the age of victorious redemption. He delivers *from* suffering but not *by means of* suffering.

III. The Post-Biblical Period

In spite of the wariness of the religious leaders, Messianic speculation and calculation has persisted in Judaism until recent times. Periods of historical change and crisis, such as the end of the Roman Empire, the Arab conquests, the Crusades, the invasions of the Ottoman Turks, and the Christian religious wars in Europe, have stimulated Jewish Messianic prospects. The time of the Messiah's coming was often computed from Biblical texts—above all, from the cryptic-number passages in Daniel (chs. 7:25; 8:14; 9:24; 12:11–12). This method was supplemented by gematria. This was a system whereby one attached numerical values to letters, and thus computed dates from virtually any Biblical verse. Astrology was also employed. A succession of Messianic pretenders or claimants to the role of Messianic forerunner, either self-designated or acclaimed by others, runs through the centuries. The stories of men such as Moses of Crete (fifth century), Abu Isa al-Ispahani, of Persia (eighth century), David Alroy, of Babylon (twelfth century), Abraham Abulafia, of Sicily (thirteenth century), Moses Botarel, of Spain (late fourteenth and early fifteenth centuries), and Solomon Molko, of Portugal (sixteenth century), corroborate beyond doubt the manifold forms that Messianism has assumed.

Many of the aspirants from the thirteenth century onward were stirred by the mystical interests of Kabbalism and did not attempt to seize political power but depended upon teaching and miracle. The high point of Messianism was reached in the seventeenth century when thousands of Jews in Europe declared Shabbethai Zebi, a Polish Jew, to be Messiah. Under duress he subsequently accepted Islam. But others after him claimed to be one of the two Messiahs and even an incarnation of Shabbethai Zebi himself. The movement continued for a century and only subsided when Kabbalism declined and Hasidism assumed more prominence. Hasidism is strongly motivated by Messianic ideals, but in contrast to Kabbalism permits virtually no calculation. For Christians, Shabbatism is of particular interest because it represents the one Messianic claim besides that of Jesus of Nazareth which continued after the death of the claimant.

The nineteenth century saw Messianic stirrings when a Yemenite Jew, Judah bar-Shalom, declared himself the forerunner Elijah, and later a man claimed to be the resurrected Judah bar-Shalom and won a wide following in Arabia, Egypt, and Palestine. Many who did not name a Messiah were, nevertheless, expecting him in such popular Messianic years as 1840, 1860, and 1866. The rapid extension of the Enlightenment and the Zionist movement culminating in the establishment of the State of Israel in 1948 have drained away much of the older enthusiasm for a Messiah. Nonetheless, the belief persists in Orthodox circles, and the large eschatological hope, of which Messianism is merely one expression, continues without abatement wherever Judaism is taken seriously as a religion.

Chapter Five

THE "ADVANTAGE" OF THE JEW

The preceding chapter was largely factual in content. Consequently, it was not of a controversial nature, as was Chapter 2. The present chapter, however, once again is an expression of the Christian interpretation of certain basic theological issues. It is concerned with the area handled by the Jewish writers Joseph Klausner, in his *From Jesus to Paul* (Beacon Press, 1961), and H. J. Schoeps, in his *Paul: The Theology of the Apostle in the Light of Jewish Religious History* (The Westminster Press, 1961), that is to say, an area of great disagreement between Jew and Christian. In this chapter, Prof. Jakob Jocz gives an exposition of Pauline teaching on Jewish-Christian relations. It will read strangely only to those Jews who are unacquainted with the recent works of Jewish and Christian scholars in New Testament studies.

—*The Editor*

Had Paul's letter to the Romans never been written, there would hardly be a theological problem for the church regarding the Jews. Even so, Christians soon came to look upon the fall of Jerusalem in A.D. 70 as the end of Jewish history. For the church, subsequent Jewish survival frequently appeared as an anachronism with no further significance to the story of redemption. It is mainly because the letter to the Romans is part of the canon of Scripture that the Jewish question is still an open one. There is thus a good excuse for introducing the problem of Jewish advantage in a theological discussion.

The idea of advantage as applied to one particular people stands opposed to a basic Christian principle for which Paul fought as no one else has, namely, that there is no difference between man and man in the sight of God. It is, therefore, somewhat of a paradox that the idea of a special Jewish advantage has Paul as protagonist. But for this fact, the church would have good reason to overlook the Jews from the very start. The original antagonism between Hebrew Christianity and the Pharisaic party created an atmosphere of hostility which not only persisted but grew with the centuries. The tendency within Gentile Christianity was to cut loose from the Jewish moorings. Marcion's opposition to the Old Testament[1] was a symptom of a universal trend. Though the church repudiated Marcion and declared him a heretic, and even retained the Old Testament as part of her Bible, in her theological thinking she distanced herself from historic Israel and drifted from the Hebrew tradition.

It is largely due to Pauline influence that in spite of strained relationships the church did not entirely lose sight of the Jewish people and clung to the hope of their ultimate salvation. Not only did Paul hold out hope that in the end "all Israel will be saved" (Rom. 11:26), "for God has the power to graft them in again" (Rom. 11:23), but what is more surprising is that even to the unbelieving Jews of his own time Paul assigned a position of preeminence.

I. Pauline "Inconsistency"

That in the context of Biblical revelation the Hebrew people occupies a unique position, no one contradicts. But the same position is denied to the Jews by reason of their rejection of the Messiah. The church understands herself as having entered upon Israel's inheritance. She worships the God of Israel; she appropriated the Bible; she identifies

[1] E. C. Blackman, *Marcion and His Influence* (London: S.P.C.K., 1950), especially Ch. 7, "Marcion and the Old Testament."

herself with the history of the Hebrew people; she claims to be the inheritor of the promises to Israel. Thus the Jewish people as the historic link between the periods before and after the birth of Christ has become redundant.

We have here a straightforward case of displacement, and there would have been little difficulty except for the testimony of Paul. For some hidden reason, he refuses to surrender the Jewish advantage and holds on to their prerogative as God's people, though this completely contradicts all his other statements. Here is a puzzle for the Christian theologian, and it is no wonder that the apostle to the Gentiles is suspected of an inconsistency.

On the one hand, Paul insists with all the vehemence of his fiery nature that God is not the God of the Jews only, but also the God of the Gentiles (Rom. 3:29). He knows only too well that the God of Israel is no respecter of persons: "You have no excuse, O man, whoever you are" (Rom. 2:1–3). But on the other hand, he not only raises the question of the Jewish advantage but also affirms it with every emphasis: "Then what advantage has the Jew? Or what is the value of circumcision? Much in every way" (Rom. 3:1–2).

This strange inconsistency is a crux to commentators. C. H. Dodd avoids the idea of advantage by translating more literally: "Then what is the Jew's superiority?[2] What is the good of circumcision?" But the result is the same, for the answer allows no variation: "Much in every way."

Dodd admits that "the logical answer on the basis of Paul's argument" ought to have been: "None whatever!" But oddly enough it is not. He therefore suggests that Paul's Pharisaism or perhaps patriotism "was too deeply engrained for him to put right out of his mind the idea that somehow the divine covenant with mankind had a 'most favoured nation clause.' "[3] But in our view, this seems to be too simple an explanation to fit a mind as complex as that of Paul.

Paul has before him a great problem: The people whom

[2] *To perisson* (Greek), noun meaning "superiority," "preeminence."
[3] C. H. Dodd, *The Epistle of Paul to the Romans* (Harper & Brothers, 1932), p. 43.

God had chosen for his special people to declare his salvation to the ends of the earth had showed themselves faithless by rejecting the Messiah. What is, then, the status of Israel, now that the act of betrayal has taken place? Is God tied to one particular people? Is he not the Father of all mankind?

The answer the apostle gives is only too plain: "There is no distinction" (Rom. 3:22), God treats all men alike, no one can boast before him (Rom. 3:27), or claim any special privileges. The Jews are not better off, "no, not at all" (Rom. 3:9)—and yet there is an advantage in being a Jew.

What is behind this apparent inconsistency? Why does the apostle hold to Israel's advantage, when the whole trend of his argument is plainly against such a view? We believe that the answer to the problem is connected with two presuppositions that underlie Pauline theology: the nature of God and the nature of history.

II. The Nature of God

The Bible sharply differentiates between God and idols. Idols cannot be trusted, but the God of Israel is the "ever-faithful One" (*el emunah,* Deut. 32:4). The supreme expression of *God's* faithfulness is to be seen in his loyalty to the covenant. For us who are reared in a different tradition, the concept of the covenant between God and Israel fails to convey an essential feature. A covenant to us is a mutual pact or agreement between two parties. But the Old Testament covenant does not involve two equal partners: God and Israel do not reach an understanding after a period of bargaining. Both the initiation of the covenant and the choice of Israel are solely a free decision on the part of God. The token and sign of God's unchanging character is to be found in the covenant. References to God's faithfulness, specially in the Psalter, relate to the covenant relationship: "Let the heavens praise thy wonders, O Lord, thy *faithfulness* in the assembly of thy saints"[4] (Ps. 89:5).

[4] The RSV translates *qedoshim* literally as "the holy ones," but this is a pedantic way of describing the assembly of God's people. Dr. R. K.

The context of this psalm is God's covenant with David, which is only another aspect of his covenant relationship to Israel. Biblical piety is nourished by the conviction that God's "loving-kindness endures forever and his *faithfulness* from generation to generation" (Ps. 100:5).

The evangelical character of Old Testament faith is tested at the point of man's failure: What happens to the covenant promises if Israel breaks her part of the vow? The Old Testament provides several answers to this question, but the most striking one it has put in the mouth of a Gentile prophet: "God is not man, that he should lie, or a son of man, that he should repent. Has he said, and will he not do it? Or has he spoken, and will he not fulfill it?" (Num. 23:19). That God's mercy goes beyond his wrath is the greatest achievement of Old Testament faith. Though God does not clear the guilty and visits the iniquity of the fathers upon the children and the children's children, yet he remains "a God merciful and gracious, slow to anger, and abounding in steadfast love and faithfulness" (Ex. 34:6). The Old Testament knows only too well, "If the Lord were to mark iniquity, who could stand?" (Ps. 130:3). The prophet Hosea is perhaps the most noble example of the Old Testament witness to the nature of God. Amid all the pronouncements of judgment, here compassion always gains the upper hand: "How can I give you up, O Ephraim! How can I hand you over, O Israel! . . . My heart recoils within me, my compassion grows warm and tender" (Hos. 11:8). These are words addressed by God to a people "bent on turning away" from him (cf. v. 7) and deserving of punishment. But God refuses to execute his fierce anger, and in order not to compromise with his obligation of justice, he refrains from entering the city: "For I am God and not man, the Holy One in your midst; therefore, I will not enter the city" (i.e., to destroy you) (ch. 11:9).

Harrison's "divine conclave" is closer to the meaning of the text. Cf. Norlie's *Simplified New Testament* with *The Psalms for Today* (Zondervan Publishing House, 1961).

Paul's concept of God was not different from that of the Old Testament. For him the gospel was the proclamation of the triumph of God's love in Christ Jesus. To say, therefore, that Israel was rejected by reason of her faithlessness would not only contradict the inner meaning of the gospel but malign God's character.

The knowledge that God is unchanging and true to his purpose is not peculiarly a Pauline achievement. Malachi 3:6 had already put it into words long before the apostle's time. The Letter of James speaks in a similar context about the Father of lights, with whom there is no variation or shadow due to turning (James 1:17). But II Tim. 2:11–13 deserves special notice. Most scholars are agreed that the passage is part of an ancient Christian hymn. Because of an affinity in language with Rom. 6:3 f., it is suggested that this was a hymn used at baptismal occasions.[5] Here, as in the case of Ps. 18:26, we meet with the typical Biblical admonition: "If we deny him, he will deny us." This may be an allusion to a word of the Lord Jesus: "Whosoever shall be ashamed of me and of my words, of him shall the Son of man be ashamed" (Luke 9:26). But the text in II Tim. 2:13 immediately proceeds with what looks like a correction: "If we are faithless, he remains faithful—for he cannot deny himself."

Against James Moffatt, E. F. Scott insists that this last sentence is not an addition or correction on the part of the writer but belongs to the quotation of the ancient hymn, and is quite in the spirit of the rest of the poem. When placed in the context of Biblical faith, E. F. Scott's contention is well justified. Right through the Old and the New Testament we meet this paradox: judgment against disloyalty and at the same time the triumph of God's grace which transcends man's failure. If it were otherwise, there would only be law but no gospel.

This is exactly the Pauline position: "What if some became unfaithful? Does their faithlessness annul the faithful-

[5] E. F. Scott, *The Pastoral Epistles,* Moffatt New Testament Commentary (Harper & Brothers, 1936), p. 105.

ness of God?" (Rom. 3:3). To this there can be only one answer: "Never! God remains the faithful one, though everyone else becomes false" (Rom. 3:4). This is an echo of Old Testament piety which is equally "Pauline." "He does not deal with us according to our sins, nor requite us according to our iniquities." (Ps. 103:10.) That God is greater than man's conscience is a fundamental tenet of Biblical faith: even when our own hearts condemn us, "God is greater than our hearts and knows everything" (I John 3:20). This kind of God is not swayed by the fickleness of man. He remains true to his Word and faithful to his purpose. If such is the case, the Pauline conclusion is the only possible one: "The gifts and calling of God are irrevocable" (Rom. 11:29). It means that Israel remains Israel in spite of herself.

III. The Nature of History

Most scholars recognize that the Biblical view of history is peculiarly its own. It is closely connected with its view of God both as sovereign Lord and as merciful Father. Because God wills history, history has a purpose. *Heilsgeschichte,* i.e., purposeful history in which all events converge to form a meaningful pattern, is rooted in a faith which assumes that God is not only sovereign but also wise. But neither sovereignty nor wisdom carry the guarantee that the goal which history pursues is to man's ultimate advantage. God, though all-powerful and all-wise, may yet use man for his own inscrutable ends; or else he may play with man's destiny as in Greek mythology. The assurance that man is not mocked and that the drama of human life has a happy ending cannot be founded upon God's power or his wisdom but solely upon his goodness. That God is the all-merciful One is not merely an assumption but the experience of Biblical man under the covenant. This is the witness of the Bible.

Biblical revelation is therefore not rooted in creation as an act of God's sovereignty, but, rather, in salvation as the expression of his loving will. Although the Bible knows God as the great potter who molds the clay according to his sovereign will (cf. Jer. 18:6; Isa. 64:8), yet he deals with his people on a strictly personal basis. He does not just handle man as a master does his slave, but speaks to his conscience as a father to his son. But the Old Testament knows of an even more intimate relationship than father to son; and this is the relation of husband to wife as the figure of God's relation to his people. This figure is largely used by the prophet Hosea to describe God's faithfulness toward his faithless people. The extent of God's limitless love is portrayed in the cross: God goes to the uttermost limit in his concern for man. In the cross man is primarily faced, not with the sovereign Lord, but with the loving Father who gives his Son for the salvation of mankind. Ultimately, therefore, it would seem that in Biblical perspective the principle of victory is defeat for love's sake. The cross expresses the most radical revaluation of values. God here allows himself to be defeated so that not his power but his love shall triumph.

The Biblical pattern of God-directed history is woven upon the canvas of God's love. The very idea of election is an expression of God's free love. His choice of Israel is neither caprice nor the reward of merit: "It was not because you were more in number than any other people that the Lord set his love upon you and chose you, for you were the fewest of all peoples; but it is because the Lord loves you, and is keeping the oath which he swore to your fathers" (Deut. 7:7–8).

True love can have no reason; it cannot depend upon the object of love, but only upon the lover. The cause is in God and not in Israel's worth or status. In spite of the fact that the Jews are the enemies of God as regards the gospel, "as regards election they are beloved for the sake of their forefathers" (Rom. 11:28).

Reference to the Patriarchs is reference to *Heilsgeschichte*, which begins with the call to Abram to leave his father's house and to become a pilgrim in quest of the Promised Land (Gen. 12:1 ff.). It is God who initiates the story and directs it.

The *sui generis* character of Hebrew history is revealed only when seen backward. We are here confronted with a small people in a barren corner of the Arabian desert, playing a part in world history out of all proportion to its size and culture. In this respect, Hebrew history is a remarkable phenomenon; it points beyond itself as does the history of no other people. Only in the sphere of the God-man relationship is the Hebrew contribution unequaled. In the realms of philosophy, art, and culture, Israel's achievements are easily dwarfed by other nations. But where moral values and spiritual insights are concerned, no other people has ever played a similar part. Oddly enough, the Hebrew contribution to the life of nations is mainly connected with one single collection of literature which we call the Holy Bible. Outside the area of Scripture the vast accumulation of Rabbinic literature is of little import to the world. The Mishnah, the Gemara, the Midrashim, the Rabbinic codes, are of small account in the shaping of world history. Only the Bible, whose history runs parallel to the history of the Hebrew people, has profoundly affected the course of mankind. What is the secret of its amazing influence?

There is a "humanistic" and an "orthodox" answer to this question. The humanist will naturally point to the moral values, ethical standards, deep insights into human nature, etc., that make the Bible such a fascinating book. The orthodox Christian will fall back upon the authority of the Bible as the word of God. Both perceptions are not necessarily exclusive, but rather complementary. There is, however, one more aspect peculiar to the Bible, and this is its understanding of history.

Within the Western tradition there is a latent tendency to approach life by way of induction from the particular to the general. We thus constantly reduce singular events to general principles. The unique, the unrepeatable, the irreversible, we therefore experience as recalcitrant material. In our effort to force the singular into a universal mold we lose the meaning of the uniqueness of events. What is universal is circular and therefore repeatable. In this case the same law or principle would apply to any number of instances. History as repetition is without a goal. For the Bible, history is a linear movement with a definite purpose in view. Here, events are irreversible and never twice the same. Every person, every occurrence, every instance in time, is endowed with a significance peculiarly its own. Here all forces, all events, all actors, cooperate to work out God's eternal purpose. Good and evil, light and darkness, war and peace, alike are factors in the great pattern of God's design. Even "the free *nihilation* of the human will," as Jacques Maritain puts it,[6] is utilized by the wisdom of God to reveal the depth of his mercy.

In this pattern of purposeful events, each particular instance derives its significance from the fact of its uniqueness. Because Biblical history is essentially Messianic history, every success and every failure, every victory and every defeat—the whole cast, individually and collectively, consciously or unconsciously, contribute to the completion of God's eternal purpose. As events are not interchangeable, so are actors irreplaceable. Each particular person and each people somehow acts out his part even when unwilling to cooperate.

The discovery of purposeful history has relieved man of meaningless circular existence and has brought new zest into life. In the Biblical perspective, there are no fortuitous happenings; there is no chance, no fate, no accident. Even the insignificant instances of daily life are built into God's mighty purpose.[7] Here every individual has a name with a meaning, a history with a purpose, and a significance that is irreplaceable. Human life takes place in a threefold context: personal life within the family; family life within the nation; national life among the nations. These histories converge and ultimately make up the meaningful pattern of God's purpose.

In this all-inclusive story of the human race, every individual, every family, and every nation plays a specific part.

[6] J. Maritain, *On the Philosophy of History* (Charles Scribner's Sons, 1957), p. 90.

[7] Cf. J. Jocz, *The Spiritual History of Israel* (London: Methuen & Co., Ltd., 1961), pp. 125 f.

Israel's task is not self-chosen; it is God who chooses and assigns responsibilities: "The Lord your God has chosen you to be a special people unto him" (Deut. 14:2); no one therefore can exchange with Israel or relieve her of her task. Israel's history is built into God's predetermined design, and because history is irreversible, Israel stands where God has placed her.

Jewish advantage must therefore be seen in the light of these two basic presuppositions: God's unfailing faithfulness and the irreversible nature of history.

IV. The Nature of Israel's Advantage

Thus far we have attempted to show the underlying presuppositions behind Paul's persistence in his claim of Israel's unique position. We have now to define the nature of the advantage the Jew enjoys. "What advantage has the Jew? Or what is the value of circumcision?" (Rom. 3:1).

The apostle gives an immediate answer, but it is incomplete; at a later stage he will augment it. His first answer is that "to the Jews are entrusted the oracles of God" (Rom. 3:2). But this is better described as a responsibility than as an advantage. The later answer is more complete: "They are Israelites, and to them belong the sonship, the glory,[8] the covenants, the giving of the law, the worship, and the promises; to them belong the patriarchs, and of their race, according to the flesh, is the Christ" (Rom. 9:4 f.). Here we have an enumeration of privileges that the apostle would put on the list of Israel's special advantage. It appears that for Paul to be born a Jew is no small prerogative: "the sonship, the glory, the covenants, the . . . law, the worship, and the promises," are all aspects of a spiritual tradition that no one dares take for granted. To be born a son of Abraham, though physical descent in itself is of no value (cf. Rom. 2:28 f.),

[8] Delitzsch correctly associates *doxa* with *shekinah*—God's gracious condescension to dwell amid his people. See Ch. 7, p. 113, of this volume. F. Delitzsch, *Paulus der Apostels Brief an die Römer* (1870), p. 88.

carries a privilege that the Gentile does not enjoy. What kind of privilege is it?

To answer the question we have to fall back once again on the importance of history in the Hebrew perspective. Election in the Bible is not just a pious phrase but carries with it a whole complex of concrete values in terms of culture and nationhood. To be born and live among God's people means to partake of the atmosphere, the tradition and values, that are the deposits of God's grace and providence. This heritage is transmissible from father to son and has persisted in Israel to this day.

The positive values that the Jewish people have derived from the Torah have preserved them and kept them buoyant in their darkest hours. Christians frequently criticize Judaism for its legalistic tendencies but fail to see the other side of the picture.

In retrospect, as one looks upon Jewish history since the fall of Jerusalem in A.D. 70, one cannot help marveling at the visible signs of Jewish advantage. The last two thousand years of dispersion present a nightmare of suffering and humiliation never equaled in history. By all the laws of reason this people ought either to have disintegrated and disappeared or else sunk to the level of pariahs. Instead, they have emerged from the holocaust unbroken in spirit, conscious of their dignity, and with a sense of mission and purpose.

The awareness of Israel's election has never left the Jewish people. Even nonbelieving Jews regard themselves as members of a *special* people. That Israel is an *'am segullah,* God's special property (cf. Ex. 19:5, and see Chapter 2), persists as the collective consciousness of the Jews. In the Hebrew liturgy, Israel's election is reaffirmed in the frequently repeated sentence: *attah beḥartanu mikkol ha'ammim*—"Thou hast chosen us from all the nations."[9] This sense of vocation carries a dignity that finds expression in all aspects of Jewish life.

[9] Cf. J. Jocz, *A Theology of Election* (London: S.P.C.K., 1958), pp. 39 f.

Though study of the Torah is in the center of Jewish piety, the purpose of such study is the keeping of the commandments. The 613 mitzvoth encompass every aspect of human life and regulate all relationships. The genius of Judaism and its strength lie in the all-pervasive emphasis upon moral values. "Not learning but doing is the chief thing," said Simeon, the son of Rabban Gamaliel (Pirke Aboth I. 17). Herein he expressed the conviction of his father, who said: "All study of Torah without work must in the end be futile and become the cause of sin" (*ibid.,* II. 2). This emphasis upon translating the law into deeds has had a sanctifying effect upon the individual and the community. Ritual cleanliness and personal hygiene were never separated and were looked upon as necessary for the hallowing of God's holy name, and Jewish marriage laws have preserved the purity of family life and have erected a bulwark against incest, sexual perversity, and adultery at times when these were commonplace among Gentiles. It is enough to read Clement of Alexandria to realize the difference between a people governed by Torah and a people under no moral restraint.[10] The cohesion of the Jewish family is the envy of the Gentiles.

Its strength comes from a long tradition of devotion to moral values. Even in this harassed age of moral decadence, the Jewish family seems to be weathering the storm better than Gentile families do. This is probably due to the fact that by custom it is not the synagogue but the home that is the center of religious life. It is an uplifting experience to observe a religious Jewish family celebrate Sabbaths, festivals, anniversaries, and family occasions in the home. Rabbi Ignaz Maybaum, in his charmingly written book *The Jewish Home* (James Clarke & Co., Ltd., London, 1946), gives a glimpse of the remarkable transformation that takes place in a Jewish home on Sabbath eve. The Hebrew siddur (prayer book) contains treasures of spirituality and religious poetry that for centuries have nourished the Jewish soul.

[10] Cf. Clement of Alexandria, *Paedagogus* II, 10; III, 3, 4, 5.

The focal point of the Jewish family is the child, particularly the male child. Love of children is a characteristic Jewish trait. The psalmist reveals himself a true Hebrew when he pronounces: "Happy is the man who has his quiver full of them!" (Ps. 127:5). Children are a gift of God, and a childless marriage is a calamity in Jewish eyes. No sacrifice is too great for Jewish parents in the bringing up and the education of their children. *Derek ereṣ,* "good manners," is a subject frequently discussed by the ancient rabbis and still plays an important part in Jewish upbringing of children. Traditionally, religious instruction begins as soon as a child is able to speak. As he grows, he becomes increasingly involved in the performance of religious duties. He becomes a fully responsible son of the law (*bar mitzvah*) at the age of thirteen. The *Bar Mitzvah* celebration is a great occasion in the Jewish community.

A fascinating vestige of Biblical influence upon the Jewish mind is the passion for social justice. The Biblical concern with society has penetrated deeply into the recesses of the Jewish conscience. This may be partly due to the minority position of the Jewish people, but it seems to us that there is more to it than the cry of the underdog. This will explain why so many Jews are involved in philanthropy and good causes. There is probably no other community, except perhaps the Society of Friends, that is equally concerned for the welfare of humanity.

It is no condescension to remark for the enlightenment of Christians, who may know little about their Jewish neighbors, that the liberality of Jews is prodigious. A survey throughout the United States conducted by the American Jewish Community brought to light this interesting fact: "In the typical community about two thirds of the respondents said that 'supporting all humanitarian causes' was essential to being a good Jew while only one third thought that 'supporting Jewish philanthropies' 'was essential to being a good Jew.' "[11]

[11] Marshall Sklare, "Commentary," November, 1962, p. 424.

In the same manner it should be emphasized that the majority of Jews make the most law-abiding citizens. The Jewish community shows the smallest proportion of delinquents, alcoholics, and drug addicts. On the other hand, Jews have an unusually high representation in the professions, at the universities, and in music, the theater, and journalism.

V. The Danger of Success

There is a paradox about moral life: success can be turned into defeat if it becomes a source of pride. This is the greatest snare to the synagogue. Roland B. Gittelsohn, writing about "Judaism and Mental Health," says: "I believe, for the overwhelming majority of Christians—the soil has been prepared for a devastating sense of self-deprecation."[12] He regards the doctrine of original sin and the moral perfection of Jesus as disturbing factors that confront the believer with an "intolerably painful dilemma." He completely overlooks the sense of forgiveness and the experience of God's gracious acceptance of sinners for Christ's sake as the essence of Christian living. But his remark points to a persistent fact: Judaism does not encourage "self-deprecation." The defeat of God for love's sake as demonstrated by the cross is a foreign, even sacrilegious concept to Judaism. The result is a different ethos, a different attitude, and a completely different perception of life and God. The basis for this statement we shall examine in the following chapter.

Yet Jews know of grace as Christians do, but they know it differently. The peculiar emphasis upon man's ability to keep the law, the insistence upon the commandments, the intense concern for ethics, make it easier for them to fall into the error of merits before God than is the case with Christians. But the church has not escaped the temptation; neither have Christians individually always managed to live by grace and not by works. Reliance upon merit on the part of fallen man seems to be deeply ingrained in human nature. The drive for

[12] "Judaism," Fall, 1959, p. 325.

self-assertion and racial superiority is as common among Christians as it is among Jews. Pride of ancestry, race, and color are bedeviling human relationships in all ages. When Paul spoke of the Jewish advantage, he did not appeal to pride of race or cultural achievement. He appealed to God's mercy and his free love in choosing an otherwise unworthy people to serve his eternal purpose with mankind. But because to serve God is man's greatest privilege, and because God's calling is historically conditioned, there is an advantage in being a Jew even today. It is the advantage of the firstborn in relation to his younger brothers. The problem of the elder brother in the parable of the prodigal son is the problem of Israel in relation to the Gentiles. It is the problem of the privileged in relation to mankind. Israel has failed in her duty and has misunderstood her vocation because man always fails. Israel's problem is thus a warning and challenge to the church. It is the warning that election may result in failure unless we translate our advantage in terms of responsibility and love. But we must never forget that human failure does not annul God's purpose with mankind. Even the wrath of man he turns to his praise. (Ps. 76:10.)

Chapter Six

THE "ADVANTAGE" OF THE CHRISTIAN

We continue with the quotation from Paul's letter to the Romans (Rom. 3:1) that is referred to in the title of Chapter 5. But this time we use it in reverse. It is natural that the Christian should believe that he has an advantage over others if he accepts his faith as true. Such a belief is basic to Judaism.

But as the reader progresses in this chapter, he will find that its author, Prof. Harold Floreen, does not deal with the issue in the way the reader probably expected he would. For the advantage of the Christian is just this unique relationship he has with the Jewish people! Professor Floreen has had deep and intimate friendships with thoughtful Jewish rabbis and laymen throughout his career. He and they together have experienced profound enrichment through their continuing dialogue with each other.

—*The Editor*

As the theme of this chapter suggests, the presentation is intended to be complementary to the preceding chapter concerning the advantage of the Jew. Unfortunately, the term "advantage" when employed in a discussion of one's own household of faith suggests a clear invitation to self-righteousness and arrogance. Paul's eloquent brief in the letter to the Romans (3:2; 9:4–5) setting forth the advantage of the Jew reminds us that our present discussion must do something other than minimize the Chosen People and their God-given role.

An objective analysis of the comparative advantages of the two faiths is extremely difficult to achieve. Advantages are best known and understood by those living within a given situation. Hence, Paul's personal experience both as a Jew and as a Christian undoubtedly accounts for the breadth of his grasp in recognizing and appreciating values on both sides. His presentation, to be sure, is not acceptable to Jews, but Paul cannot be accused of oversimplifying the issues. In this volume, the choice has been to deal with the respective advantages of Jew and Christian in separate chapters. Hence, it is hoped that the reader will keep the previous presentation in mind as he considers the development of the present theme.

At the outset it should be stated that any boasting or arrogance on the part of the Christian is particularly inappropriate in the light of his indebtedness to the Jews. Though not spoken in this context, two questions which Paul addressed to the Corinthians would be most fitting here: "What have you that you did not receive? If then you received it, why do you boast as if it were not a gift?" (I Cor. 4:7). The Christian is the recipient of the fruit of generations of toil and suffering on the part of Israel.

I. Advantages in Communication and Reconciliation

In their contacts with Jews, Christians have a number of advantages. Unfortunately, those advantages remain largely unrecognized, at least in practice. Taboos, such as those which limit traditional Jews in their social relationships with non-Jews, either do not exist for Christians or are of minor social significance. Jewish festival and ceremonial, which play an extremely important role in Jewish faith and worship, involve little that should be offensive to the Christian. Rather, there is much that is to be admired in those aspects of Judaism and that could be meaningful to Christians, representing as they do values and events which are organically related to the Christian heritage. Why should we not rejoice, for example, at Hanukkah, the Feast of Dedication? Victory of the Jews over the Syrian Greeks, who were trying to force them into idolatry, and the rededication of the Temple, which the enemy had desecrated, were events as vital to the future of Christianity as to that of Judaism. Possibly the only celebration that would seem strange to the Christian would be that of Purim with its noisemaking and the cursing of Haman. With a more developed doctrine of final judgment, Christians would be content to let God take care of Haman. Again, the Jewish prayer book is a noble creation with heavy Scriptural content and with comparatively little that would offend a Christian. Jews, on the other hand, have much greater difficulty in finding themselves at home with Christian customs and practices.

The Christian belief that righteousness is not an inherent quality of the natural man, but is a gift from God, provides a potentially favorable climate for self-criticism, which is much more difficult to practice when one feels it necessary to affirm one's own righteousness. An honest expression of guilt and penitence on the part of one party in a controversy, especially if it be the chief offender, is a necessary beginning and a vital step toward reconciliation and understanding.

Again, the Christian emphasis upon reconciliation and forgiveness, *if* carried out in practice, affords an advantage in rectifying relationships with one's Jewish brother. In the light of the sufferings and persecutions endured by the Jews, it seems strange to speak of Christians showing a spirit of forgiveness toward them. It is important, however, to realize that it is frequently the most guilty party who finds it difficult to forgive. It is a terrible indictment that the spirit of reconciliation has so often been lacking in our relationships with Jewish people.

That Christians are the majority group in most localities in North America puts them at an advantage in showing neighborliness and brotherly love. People of a minority group, especially if it is quite small, often hesitate to take the initiative.

One of the greatest advantages the Christian discovers in communicating with the Jew is the Jew himself. Much as the Jew declares that the degree to which Jesus stressed love is impractical, no one is more responsive than he to such love when it is actually practiced. The approach of love finds him warmhearted, responsive, and very personal in his interest, so that he recognizes and responds to goodwill even if there is disagreement at the intellectual level. A keen sense of justice and fair play enables him quickly to recognize sincerity and integrity in another and often causes him to defend the right of the other to voice honest conviction, even though he might disagree with the substance of that conviction. Fairness requires it to be said that, in the long run, he who blesses the Jew is truly blessed. It is God who has promised to bless those who bless Abraham, but many a Jew seems to feel that it is his personal responsibility to assist God in carrying out his promise.

One sometimes hears a Christian say that he has had little or no opportunity for personal contact with Jewish people. If there is a representative number of Jewish people in the area, the person making such a comment reveals the limited extent of his interest in the general well-being of his community. Through a passion for justice in public affairs, a keen interest in efforts to alleviate suffering and need, and a consistent effort to further the progress of public education and of worthwhile cultural development, Jewish people generally provide numerous situations in which Christians can meet them and work with them in worthy endeavors that violate no Christian principles. Lack of contact is generally not the fault of the Jews.

II. The Advantage in Appreciation

As previously stated, Christians should regard it an advantage to be the recipients and beneficiaries of the fruits of the incalculable toil and suffering of the Jews over a period of centuries. Still further, they have the high privilege of bringing to the nations the benefits of God's revelation and redemption which came through the Jews. This is not an inconsequential task, nor is it a privilege bereft of toil and suffering.

A certain polarity between Christian and Jew in the human situation is not all evil in that it gives the Christian a significant advantage, provided that the polarity is not permitted to obscure the existence of a more fundamental unity. For example, if the Christian is willing to acknowledge with Paul that, before God, all attempts to draw sharp distinctions between men in terms of righteousness or of sinfulness are hypocritical, then he is on the way to discovering in the Jew an alter ego through whom he can come to understand himself. That the penitential psalms, which grew out of Jewish experience, are as universally and as beneficially used among Christians as among Jews is an acknowledgment, at least in practice, of the reality of this truth. The unfortunate tendency, however, on the part of many Christians to limit their sense of kinship only to the Hebrews of Old Testament times indicates a failure to understand the solidarity of Israel which transcends time. It is precisely the presence of Jews in our midst today that keeps the relationship from becoming anachronistic.

The self-understanding that the Christian thus gains through the Jew must be regarded as a tremendous advantage, and not least because it comes gratuitously. To make this advantage possible for the Christian, the Jews paid a fearful price. The frank confession of that which they had learned concerning themselves in the presence of God and in the maelstrom of history and which they courageously recorded for anyone to read became a mirror of priceless worth for the entire race (I Cor. 10:1–12). At the same time, it provided the best possible ammunition for the persecutors of the Jews throughout the ages.

The Christian has a great advantage also in possessing the testimony of the Hebrew Scriptures to God's abiding goodness and faithfulness to his people. Through the polarity that exists between Christian and Jew, the Christian can see in his own experience, and especially in that of the church on a worldwide scale, a corroborating witness to the primary testimony of the Jews. The survival of both Israel and the church to this day has been nothing short of miraculous through the grace of God. Again, this advantage of a double witness has come gratuitously. Its effect should be the glorification of God, and its very antithesis should be our repudiation of kinship with the Jews as objects of divine grace.

Finally, the Christian's advantage in the grounds he possesses for an appreciation of the Jew has not only a past reference but also a present and a future reference. The contention of some Christians that the Jews no longer possess a unique role in God's purposes has no Scriptural basis or support. The New Testament, indeed, holds that a Jewish monopoly upon acceptance as children of God no longer exists, but this was anticipated centuries earlier by the prophet Isaiah, who declared that one day the Lord would claim both Egypt and Assyria as his people along with Israel (ch. 19:24–25). The elimination of any place for a special role for Israel is based by some on the words of Paul in Gal. 3:28–29: "There is neither Jew nor Greek, there is neither slave nor free, there is neither male nor female; for you are all one in Christ Jesus. And if you are Christ's, then you are Abraham's offspring, heirs according to promise."

A careful study of the above passage will indicate that Paul is speaking of divine acceptance, but not of vocation. Otherwise, the differentiated functions of male and female likewise would have to cease. Far from depreciating Israel's unique role in God's Kingdom, Paul anticipated that someday it would be revived with great blessing (Rom. 11:11–12, 28–29). It becomes an advantage to the Christian that his New Testament Scriptures, far from calling upon him to ignore or despise the Jews in terms of the present and future, instead bid him to appreciate and respect them as possessing a divine calling or vocation that is irrevocable (Rom. 11:28–29).

III. The Advantage of the Christian Gospel and of a Worldwide Mission

If it be granted that it is important that the God of Israel should become known and worshiped among the nations, it must be acknowledged that the Christian gospel possesses real advantages in the outreach to non-Jews. As a message that stresses divine grace to the exclusion of human prerogatives and merit, it precisely meets the needs of the Gentiles. To put it the other way around, Who is a better candidate for such a gospel than the Gentile who possesses neither rights, nor claims, nor prerogatives? His very lack of any claim whatsoever is a great advantage toward a humble acceptance of the grace of God. At the point, however, that the possession of God's grace causes him to boast against the Jew, he immediately forfeits his advantage (Rom. 11:17–22).

With the Jew, on the other hand, the gospel of Christ with its stress upon pure grace is an offense to his prerogatives. That a gospel of grace is irrelevant to the Jews, however, is seriously open to question in the light of such passages as Deut. 7:7–8; Isa. 48:9–11; Ezek. 20:18–22; 36:32; etc. Paul maintained, in fact, that one of the privileges of Gentile Christians who had been so enriched by the Jews would be the opportunity to share the gospel with them (Rom. 11:30–32).

The Christian gospel marked the fullest realization of two seemingly conflicting trends already observed in the prophets. There had been a narrowing or concentrating of the focus of attention from the nation to the remnant (in Isaiah), to the individual (in Jeremiah and Ezekiel). On the other hand, there had been an expanding vision of the outreach of divine salvation. For example, the Lord addressed his servant thus in Isa. 49:6:

> It is too light a thing that you should be my servant
> to raise up the tribes of Jacob
> and to restore the preserved of Israel;
> I will give you as a light to the nations,
> that my salvation may reach to the end of the earth.

It should be obvious that any outreach to mankind in general must have the entire race in view, but that it must of necessity involve the individual. It is the advantage of the Christian that the gospel entrusted to him does both of these things consummately. In John 3:16 the "world" and "whosoever" significantly appear in the same verse; and the Great Commission of Matt. 28:19–20 embraces all nations, but clearly reaches down to the individual as seen in the charge to make disciples, to baptize, and to teach.

The Christian gospel has the advantage that it touches uniquely the most deeply felt needs of the individual. To him who trusts in Christ is granted assurance of divine forgiveness and of acceptance as a child of God, gifts that result in deep inner joy and peace. There is likewise granted a sense of purpose, of vocation, and of divine guidance in life. Assurance of eternal life which transcends death brings treasured comfort to bereaved hearts; and, though too often used as an occasion for an exaggerated otherworldliness, it has resulted in countless examples of the grateful dedication of every resource and faculty to the service of God and man in the stream of everyday life.

IV. The Advantage of Having a Christ

Our discussion of the advantage of the Christian has missed the very essence of the matter if it has not focused upon the person of Jesus. In Jesus Christ the Christian has seen the compassionate face of the Heavenly Father and has become reconciled with him—the one thing that matters most for time and eternity. This has brought new life, a life so bound up with the person of Jesus that the believer can say with Paul, "For to me to live is Christ." The depth of meaning involved in that relationship can be grasped only from within the relationship. To attempt a comprehensive statement would be to write a theology of the New Testament.

Although his own life is bound up with Jesus Christ, the Christian has an advantage in standing somewhat apart from the controversy between Jesus and his people, the Jews. This affords the possibility of observing certain perspectives or facets of the problem which would very likely pass unnoticed by the Jews in the heat of the controversy. It is thought that the presentation of several of these perspectives might prove helpful in illustrating the advantage that the Christian claims to have in his understanding and possession of Jesus as the Christ.

For Israel, the exodus stands out as the primary landmark of God's redemptive activity whereby, acting in pure grace, he delivered the Hebrews from bondage and created of them a people for his own possession. A second major landmark of redemption was the return from captivity in Babylon. In this return, the prophets stressed that God was acting for his own sake alone and not on the basis of any righteousness or merit on the part of Israel. In fact, the opening message of the fortieth chapter of Isaiah was a message of gracious forgiveness. Jeremiah's comment on the relationship between these two events is instructive:

> Therefore, behold, the days are coming, says the Lord, when it shall no longer be said, "As the Lord lives who brought up the people of Israel out of the land of Egypt," but "As the Lord lives who brought up the people of Israel out of the north country and out of all the countries where he had driven them." For I will bring them back to their own land which I gave to their fathers. (Jer. 16:14–15.)

Obviously, the two events could be used interchangeably as normative of God's gracious redemptive action in behalf of his people. It should be noted, however, that the two events proved normative in the thinking of the Jews only. In each instance, a number of Gentiles indeed were attracted; and in Isa. 49:7 it was anticipated that the salvation wrought by the Lord's servant would reach to the ends of the earth. It is true that King Cyrus granted liberation also to exiled peoples other than the Jews; but, beyond that, neither event was accepted or even understood by the Gentiles as normative for their salvation.

If the salvation of the Lord were to reach the ends of the

earth, there would be needed a redemptive event that would involve the Gentiles directly as well as the Jews and that would be understood and accepted by them. It is precisely such an event that we have in the redemptive death and resurrection of Jesus Christ. As with the return from Babylon, this event stressed forgiveness and reconciliation. Forgiveness was the keynote both on the cross and in the proclamation of the apostles. As in the exodus, the Lord created for himself a people that embraced men of every nation and tongue as well as the Jews. The tents of Shem were enlarged, for Japheth had come to dwell in them. (Gen. 9:27.)

The majority of Jews have rejected the atonement of Christ as normative of God's grace to them, but millions of Gentiles through the centuries as well as many Gentile nations have seen in this event the ultimate outpouring of God's redeeming grace to all men, both Jews and non-Jews, and the assurance of the election by God of the Gentiles also as his own people. It is significant that once Gentile Christians have seen in Christ the Suffering Servant of the Lord who has borne their iniquities, they have little difficulty in understanding and appreciating what the exodus and the return from Babylon have meant to the Jews, for all three are authentic expressions of the divine grace.

Another perspective in which the Christian seems to have an advantage has to do with the nature of divine love. When God affirms that he loves his people (Jer. 31:3; etc.), what does his love imply? Love is repeatedly depicted in the Scriptures as an exchange, a free sharing with another of that which one possesses himself, together with a readiness to receive that which the other wishes to offer. If the exchange is between two who are unequal, it can be carried through on the part of the greater one only through selfless devotion and often at the cost of much sacrifice or vicarious suffering.

We see precisely such manifestation of love in the description of the Suffering Servant of the Lord in the famed "Servant passages" of Isaiah, but we also see it acted out in life around us by unselfish parents, in genuine marriages, and in many other situations. Does God love thus? If he does, can he depict it only in the agony of a Hosea? Can there be no direct involvement on his part in our burdens and guilt? Can his love be real to us as men and can it be as genuine as that of a Hosea if he himself never actually enters into our situation to make the exchange? It is the testimony of countless Christians that God actually did this in Christ and that they have experienced the healing as the Lord entered in, giving them of the riches of his grace and taking their sorrows and guilt and burdens.

V. An Embarrassing Advantage

Again, the Christian, standing somewhat apart from the issues currently confronting the Jews, might discern aspects of the problems that are not so easily seen by those immediately involved. The difficulty with this advantage is that a Christian who is at all morally sensitive finds that his own guilt has so compromised his authority to speak that his comments could easily be construed as hypocritical self-justification. The absence or relative feebleness of any protest even by Christians who opposed the Nazi persecution of the Jews has made all of us party to and guilty of the heinous crime of our own generation against that people. One still faces the moral question, however, whether such embarrassment can justify stifling observations that could serve to help rather than to destroy. Nor does the possibility of being misunderstood absolve of responsibility all who have the advantage of at least a measure of detachment. After all, a charge of anti-Semitism is not so terrifying as God's displeasure for failing to be the sort of friend who places the well-being of the other above the other's approval or acceptance.

A discerning Christian finds in the amazing modern turn of events in the history of the Jews factors that both thrill and trouble him. There is a certain fitness in Israel's coming home. In relation to God, Israel was most commonly seen in the Scriptures as a female figure, i.e., playing the role of obedience, reverence, and receptivity. Noah's words, "Blessed be the Lord, the God of Shem," anticipated this stance (Gen.

9:26). But this very receptivity and the consequent enrichment fitted Israel to assume the male role of father and benefactor to the Gentile peoples. Noah's words to the third son, "God enlarge Japheth," indeed indicated a male role for many Gentile peoples in carrying out the God-given responsibility of the race to fill the earth and to subdue it. The remainder of the promise to Japheth, however, "and he shall dwell in the tents of Shem," indicated a "female" role on the part of Gentile peoples in relation to the chosen people, for it is the male or father figure who controls the tents. Hence the return of Jews to Palestine is a return to Israel's initial role and as such a refutation of charges of an alien character on Israel's part in dwelling solely among the Gentiles.

However, there are certain disturbing features in the present situation. Strong tendencies in Israel toward a secularized society do not harmonize with a spiritual claim to the land; and a claim on any other basis is hard to substantiate. Moreover, these secular tendencies do not accord with Israel's God-given role which alone justifies her peculiar apartness as a people.

These considerations are particularly disturbing when one senses that Israel in our generation has the greatest opportunity of her history to sanctify the name of God before the world. In the same generation in which she was reconstituted as a nation in her own land, she had been sinned against as no other people in history. As would any other people, she has used her right to point out the crimes committed against her people. Anyone who is aware of the criminal attempts of not a few to deny or minimize the horrors and the injustices that rest or should rest upon the conscience of our generation with respect to the Jews will understand the objective in the Eichmann trial. It was clearly that of uncovering before the world the true story of the Nazi inferno and of permitting the victims publicly to bear their testimony. God's moral indignation over the covering up of Saul's crime in seeking, through perverted nationalistic zeal, to exterminate the Gibeonites, has something to say to us in this matter (II Sam. 21:1–14). And yet, even an open trial before the world could only be a hopelessly inadequate token of that which should be revealed. The agony of the Jews in our generation is simply beyond the possibility of human comprehension. In thus using her right, however, Israel has affirmed the right of other peoples to dramatize the wrongs that they feel have been committed against them.

Nevertheless, our principal concern at this point is the opportunity and the responsibility that still confront Israel in our day. If no generation has sinned against her as has this one, neither has any generation ever witnessed as many expressions of sorrow, repentance, and token attempts to make restitution. It is undoubtedly true that some of these expressions are possibly motivated principally by a desire to find relief from an intolerably tortured conscience; but to call them all insincere would be the height of cynicism, especially as they include expressions from not a few who come from the rising generation that had no direct involvement in the attempted genocide.

Somehow, the position of Israel at this juncture is strangely like that of Jonah at Nineveh as pictured in the Old Testament. If any non-Assyrian contemporaries had been minded to criticize Jonah's preaching, one can be sure they would have accused him of not attacking strongly enough the Assyrian violence and brutality that the Assyrian king himself freely acknowledged. In powerfully preaching divine judgment, Jonah indeed was fulfilling his God-given assignment. Wherein was he lacking? He rebelled at the thought of giving to the penitent Assyrians the complete revelation of the God of Israel, at the same time confessing that he well understood that the Lord is "a gracious God and merciful, slow to anger, and abounding in steadfast love, and repentest of evil."

Had Jonah desired to give a revelation of God's mercy to the Assyrians in proper proportion to his powerful preaching of judgment, he would have faced a most difficult task. Perhaps this is one reason why the Suffering Servant in Isaiah is pictured as remaining silent when persecuted and maltreated, for a true revelation of God's mercy would then fall within the realm of possibility.

As did Jonah, Israel today faces a magnificent opportunity as well as a most difficult task. She has suffered in our day as has no other people, she has made her just charges, and there have been many expressions of sorrow and repentance. If Israel refuses, as did Jonah, to proclaim God's unbelievable mercy to the truly penitent, she will thereby fail to express that side of the divine revelation which is by far the more significant. But to give such a revelation effectively and honestly, an act of forgiveness on Israel's part is necessary. We as Gentiles and as Christians cannot demand this of her, for forgiveness cannot be forced or legislated, especially by the guilty. In this matter, however, Israel faces her God, and her own purpose for existence as a chosen people hangs in the balance. At no other time in history could the wonder of divine forgiveness be more perfectly revealed than right now against the darkness and horror of Israel's sufferings. Prophetic voices among the Jews reveal a grasp of this situation, but more common is the assertion that it is impossible to forgive. That God forgives the penitent, even if it be a King Manasseh (see II Chron. 33:1–13), is a teaching common both to Judaism and to Christianity. If Israel refuses to forgive, will she any longer be the People of God which has been created to reveal him to the world and to sanctify his name? Again, we say, we cannot demand this forgiveness. Were it to take place, we assuredly realize, it would be a tremendous and earthshaking miracle.

To speak of these things to one's Jewish brethren is painful, as we have said, because of one's own guilt and also because it means to point once again to that "absurd" forgiveness of which the Christian first learned through Jews, but which for two thousand years has been regarded by Israel in general as unrealistic, if not actually immoral. Yet, as Israel goes forth from the "iron furnace," she carries with her the "bones of Joseph"—the bones of him who had become an unspeakable blessing to those who had wronged him, nourishing them and feeding them. Is the Christian vindictive if he is jealous for Israel's rightful role as a blessing and if he is troubled when other expressions dim that role?

Chapter Seven

BUILDING THEOLOGICAL BRIDGES

Though this double chapter is the work of the Editor of the volume, it includes in the second part a significant contribution by Frederick Neumann, Congregational minister in Brooklyn, N.Y.

The author believes that Judaism and Christianity misunderstand each other radically at two points. These are in the interpretation of the concepts of incarnation and of atonement. Yet both conceptions are to be found in that book which we have in common, viz., the Old Testament. Evidently it is a question of hermeneutics that is before us. The title of the chapter, therefore, "Building Theological Bridges," reveals the author's reconciling intention, for here he makes an attempt to express the Christian understanding of these two issues in Hebraic, rather than in Hellenic terms.

—*The Editor*

One of the tasks challenging this generation of Jews and Christians is that of building theological bridges. That both parties have actually begun to make the attempt in this present decade is one of the most heartening signs for a deeper understanding between the church and the synagogue that the world has known since the fall of Jerusalem in A.D. 70. Once the rift took place between the young church and the ancient synagogue, the church foolishly made little use of

Hebraic categories of thought to express its faith to the nations. Instead, it turned, though of necessity, to the thought forms that were more readily understandable by the Hellenistic world. That it so largely succeeded in expressing its message in contemporary Hellenistic thought forms is one of the triumphs of the human mind. But in doing so, it rendered the expression of its Christology strange and finally incomprehensible to the Jews of the second and third centuries.

The Reformation has been called the "rejudaissance" of the Christian faith, in that it reflected in part a rediscovery of the Hebraic categories of the Bible; thus the modern movement in Biblical theology is but a continuation of the same phenomenon. We shall therefore discuss here two representative ideas that till now have deeply divided us, those of incarnation and atonement. Naturally we shall do so from the Christian point of view. But we shall seek to discover whether there are any Biblical categories that can help us to begin to build bridges across the gap.

I. The Incarnation

Till recently, the Jew has prided himself that he is not a "theologian"; but today, and particularly in North America, there are those who see the need to express Judaism theologically. By this term, however, the Jew means that he is not a theologian in the Hellenic-Christian sense of the term. In the spirit of his own Old Testament, he normally describes the God of the Bible as he acts, and so as he reveals himself in his actions in the history of his people, and as he educates them to be his Servant. Thereafter he is quite content not to analyze what he has "seen," particularly not to "analyze God" as he is in himself. We are to remember that Maimonides (twelfth century) undertook to write a Jewish "theology" only as a necessary reply to the claims of the Christian church. On this basis, then, ancient Israel pictorialized a number of ways in which a man can come to "see," or have "in-sight" into, the Word becoming Event. One of the pictures that they chose to use is described by the term "Spirit."

"Spirit" and "wind" are the one and identical word in Hebrew. Now, man can see neither wind nor spirit. Yet he can see the effect of the presence of both of them. When the Old Testament speaks of God's *ruaḥ* (spirit or wind), therefore, as "moving over the face of the waters" (Gen. 1:2), or as *inspiring* life in Israel when the latter was exiled in Babylonia (Ezek., ch. 37), it does not mean to suggest that there exists some entity other than God which does these things described. Far less does it want to suggest that "spirit" is some kind of emanation from the mouth of God, as did the ancient Egyptians. Each of these phrases is, rather, a *picture,* understandable on our human level, of the God in action who is unknowable, and yet who "becomes visible" in action as Event.

When it speaks of the Glory of God, again, the Old Testament makes a parallel claim for his activity on the descriptive level that we can understand. Glory is the "visible" outer aspect of the invisible God in the act of giving himself in redeeming love. Even the heavens can be brought into use to this end, and they may declare the Glory of God. But inanimate objects cannot reveal a personal God. So that section of the Old Testament which shows the deepest insights into the ways of God declares that in some total way and in a personal manner God's Glory will be revealed in and through the people of Israel (Isa. 40:5; 49:3). God's action in this regard will then be understood not in any mechanical sense; rather, it will be revealed by means of the deepest experience and "knowledge" that man can reach, experiences which he can in fact plumb only when he meets with the buffetings of fate and is confronted in an ultimate manner by the iniquities of his fellowmen (Isa., ch. 53). Thus in a final sense it is not man as such who will plumb those depths, but God himself. For just as a husband, on the basis of his being one flesh with his wife, can suffer pains and penalties that she ought by rights to carry (Hos., chs. 1 to 3), so will God, "on that day," become "one flesh" with his Spouse, Israel (Isa. 62:5), and suffer *in her place.*

Picture theology. This "picture" theology is characteristic, then, of Hebraic thought in the Old Testament, in the New Testament, and in the Talmud alike. For example, the modern philosophical concept of the "transcendence" of God is not a Hebraic way of speaking. Rather, the Old Testament prefers to describe God even as he *acts transcendently:*

> Who hath measured out the waters in the hollow of his hand,
> And meted out heaven with a span,
> And comprehended the dust of the earth in a measure?
> (Isa. 40:12.)

In the same way, when the concept of "immanence" has to be expressed, picture language is again employed. Thus, for example, when Solomon utters his famous prayer at the dedication of the Temple, what he says is: "But will God dwell indeed on the earth? Behold, the heaven and heaven of heavens cannot contain thee; how much less this house that I have builded? Yet have thou respect unto the place of which thou hast said, My name shall be there" (I Kings 8:27–29). A man's name in Old Testament times was, ideally at least, the perfect description of its owner. So his name could even represent him almost as if he had an alter ego. If such was true of him, then, it must necessarily be true of God as well. For man has been made in the image of God.

We read in Ex., ch. 33, how the Lord talked with Moses when the latter passed through the door of the Tabernacle in the wilderness. For there the Glory of God chose to alight, even though God remained hidden by a cloud from the eye of man (Ex. 16:10). But Old Testament pictorial language is not limited to such a phrase as this. For God promised to let his Face ("presence" in the KJV, Ex. 33:14) go along with Israel in her wanderings, even while God himself remained "invisible." It is obvious that no man can see another's character or fully comprehend his real nature and being. But a man can certainly see on his friend's face all that he needs to know about him in order to enter into personal relationships with him. In this way God lets Moses know that allowing his "Face" to accompany Israel is equal to showing him his Glory (Ex. 33:18), or letting his Name be heard in their midst.

Another record within the Pentateuch offers an interesting summary of these pictorial categories. All three words, "Face," "Glory," and "Name," are necessarily impersonal *things,* although we admit that they are highly effective for pictorial purposes. What Ex. 23:20–21 does is to unify them all in the *personal* figure of an Angel. This Angel is, of course, still God, for we are meant to envisage God in action as he leads his people toward the Promised Land; but at the same time, curiously enough, this angel is distinct from God, just as his Name is distinct from him. "Behold, I send an Angel before thee, to keep thee in the way, and to bring thee into the place which I have prepared. Beware of him, and obey his voice, provoke him not; for he will not pardon your transgressions: for my Name is in him." It is God alone, of course, who can forgive sins. So this Angel is to be understood as a pictorial representation of the immanence of God in the act of revealing to Israel the forgiveness of God, even though, as we recall, no man can see God and live (Ex. 33:20). Centuries later, the prophet known as Malachi ("my angel"), we note, expects God to reveal himself within the Temple once again in the form of the Angel of the Covenant; yet he believes that when the Angel will do so, it will be none other than God himself in all his majesty who will then reveal himself as Judge (Mal. 3:1–6).

One of the most beautiful of the Hebraic pictorial images is depicted for us by the Rabbinical term "Shekinah." Though the word does not occur in the Old Testament, it stems from the good Biblical verb "to dwell." We recall that the Name, Face, Spirit, and Glory of God could each dwell, or "tabernacle" (I Kings 8:12–13; II Chron. 20:9; Ex. 29:43), in Israel's midst. Buxtorf's famous dictionary of A.D. 1622 defines the term "Shekinah" (see glossary) as *"Habitatio, divinitas, gloria, majestas divina inter homines habitans."* Buxtorf had read this word frequently in the Aramaic Targum, the translation of the Old Testament used in the synagogue in the early Christian centuries. For example, the Targum Onkelos translates Deut. 6:15 by "For the Lord thy God is a jealous God, his Shekinah dwelleth in the midst of thee." At Num. 23:21, God's Shekinah is spoken of in terms parallel with his Word. Yet, like the Angel of the Covenant of Ex., ch. 23, the Shekinah can be mentioned without any necessary association with God at all. Thus at Lev. 9:23 we read: "The Shekinah revealed itself." At Lev. 26:11 we have a number of our concepts in juxtaposition: "I will set the Shekinah of my Glory among you, and my Word shall not abhor you, but the Glory of my Shekinah shall dwell among you, and my Word shall be to you for a redeeming God and you shall be unto my Name for a holy people."

The above, then, represents an approach to the truths of the creeds in non-Hellenistic language. So the question we have before us is this: Ought not we Christians to make use of such pictorial categories with the express purpose in our mind of drawing closer to our Jewish brethren? Why should we employ only the language of the great creeds and confessions? These have been the necessary bridges between the church and the pagan world for many centuries and in many cultures. And these bridges have held against the buffetings of many a storm and earthquake. But since the Christian church is already one in covenant fellowship with those Jewish people who live in the same street as the members of its congregations, why should we not suppose that it might be possible, for love's sake, to think our thoughts about the love of God in Christ in those molds also in which the Jew, our brother, feels himself at home?

The Ontological Problem. Immediately we try to do so, however, there arises between us and our Jewish brethren the ontological problem connected with the nature of pictorial thinking. I mean, it is one thing to describe truth in pictures; it is another to describe it in terms of personality. Yet if both Jesus and the early (i.e., Jewish) church overcame this barrier (cf. Luke 24:27) by expressing the meaning of the cross and the incarnation by means of Old Testament pictorial categories alone, then it is surely incumbent upon us now to try to discover how they were able to do so.

The fact of Israel as an empirical people is, of course, no ontological problem in itself. Rather, Israel's immensely long history since the days of Abraham is a historical reality of which there is no denial. Moreover, the imagery by means of which Israel meditated upon her election and relationship to God has also persisted over the centuries.

A very early source within the Pentateuch speaks of Israel as God's firstborn son (Ex. 4:22). Of course, that designation suggests no ontological relationship between God and Israel, as it would if pagans had been speaking. As we recall, Israel is "nontheological" in her thinking. Israel liked to use images for the purpose of expressing truth. The prophets even believed that the images which formed in their mind and which they then uttered were from God; and so the images actually participated in creating the reality itself. Thus no nation on earth ever used images so daring as those which the prophets chose. In fact, some of Israel's favorite images almost verge on blasphemy. For no human mind could ever suggest or think up on its own initiative that a nation as capricious, as stiff-necked, as egocentric as the prophets declared Israel to be, could be reckoned as the Wife of the living God! Yet Hosea employs this startling figure, and Jeremiah follows him in the next century, then Ezekiel and the Second Isaiah. (It is owing to the persistence of this image that we refer to Israel as "she" more frequently than as "he.")

This imagery is not just an example of that particularism from which the philosophically-minded of the Hellenized world withdrew in disdain. Its scandal rests elsewhere. It is that Israel's relationship to God is understood as belonging within the realm of a developing purpose that God plans to reveal in and through his one and only chosen people; and it has to do with the reality that if God sets his love upon anyone or anything (for the prophets knew that God is concerned even for inanimate nature), then the ideal that he holds for that one must necessarily eventuate and become reality. That is the argument of the Isaiah of the exile about the Jerusalem which God chose to make into his dwelling (Deut. 12:11; Ps. 132:13; Isa. 2:3; 31:5; Lam. 2:1; Ezek. 43:7; Zech. 14:4); so he "pictures" God planning the rebuilding of the city in the days of exile (Isa. 49:13–17). Similarly, God's "Wife," Israel, will someday cease to be the rebellious whore that she is and become the true Bride. Moreover, this thing will certainly happen "on that day," Hos. 2:18 declares. For on that day, when God will visit Israel in person, then the parties to the marriage will be united at last. What, then, is to prevent the Christian from seeking to understand the incarnation in terms of this pictorial imagery? For, as Isa. 55:11 insists, even such a scandalous Word as this (the figure of the "marriage" of Israel with the Spirit of God) must finally become Event.

It is not difficult to realize that the language of John 1:1–18 is but a resumption of Old Testament passages. For example, Gen. 1:1–3 declares, "In the beginning . . . God said, 'Let there be light'; and there was light"—and light became Event. Again, Prov. 8:22 can say of the divine Wisdom, "The Lord possessed [or begot] me in the beginning of his way." Isaiah 55:10–11 even speaks of the Word of God as necessarily becoming Event, in the sense that the rain necessarily causes food to come out of the ground. In the light of these words, the Targum to Isa. 45:22 can interpret the sentence: "Return to me, for I have redeemed you," with "Look unto my Word, and be saved." Accordingly, Rendel Harris, in his *The Origin of the Prologue to St. John's Gospel* (Cambridge University Press, 1917) can state that the Word of God in that chapter is both the expression of the Will of God and at the same time the fulfillment of that Will, and that the latter is now identified by John with Life itself.

So then Israel, the Vine that God brought up out of Egypt and planted in the Promised Land (Ex. 15:17; Isa. 5:1–7; Jer. 2:21; Ezek., ch. 15; Ps. 80), composed, of course, of sinful men, cannot remain as such. The true Vine must eventually appear from within the stock of Israel, just as the butterfly must eventually emerge from the caterpillar whose very life blood it carries in its veins. How much more, then, must not the sinful Son, Israel, finally focus upon an Israel that will be the ideal Son? Or, to change our gender as we make reference to Israel, it is to be the Virgin Israel (rather than "Virgin of Israel," the unidiomatic translation used in the English versions for a description of Israel employed by several of the prophets) who will someday bring forth her son and sons (Isa. 66:5–13), on that day when God will begin to make all things new (v. 22).

However, we have not yet bridged the "ontological gap" between pictorial thinking and historical event. For picture language is not enough to satisfy our understanding of the astonishing reality to which we hold, viz., that the Word of God became Event at a moment in history and actually dwelt among us. Yet it is the very images of the Old Testament that can most truly help us to reach that point. One of these is the persisting view that the one who is the head or leader of a group can represent and sum up in himself the whole "personality" of that group. This was a true conception in the case of the anointed king in Jerusalem. The king was accounted the representative before God of all Israel, and all Israel was held to be present in a vital sense in its king. (See Chapter 4.) After the return from exile, when no king reigned in Jerusalem, this representative capacity of his was transferred to the person of the high priest, so that when the latter entered into the Holy of Holies, as the representative of all Israel, all Israel went in by proxy. Again, we can see how this way of thinking was understood to have a "vertical" significance as well as a "horizontal" one. A thousand years after the death of Jacob, or Israel, the whole nation could still be addressed either as Jacob or as Israel, in the singular. Now, this corporate way of thinking is essential for an understanding of the Biblical faith as a whole. For example, we notice how all Israel can make the following request of all

Edom: "Let *me,* I pray *thee,* pass through *thy* land" (Num. 20:17); or how Hosea can speak of all Israel as the "Wife" of God, and Second Isaiah declare that all Israel is the Servant of God, again in the singular. But conversely, too, one individual person can represent the whole of Israel in these capacities in question, and can speak as if he were the mouthpiece of this Israel which is viewed as a corporate entity. Thus just one singer can lament the destruction of Jerusalem, even while the whole citizenry is included in his voice: "Is it nothing to you, all you who pass by? Look and see if there is any sorrow like my sorrow" (Lam. 1:12). In the same way, while the whole nation of Israel is addressed as the Servant throughout the sixteen chapters of Second Isaiah (cf. ch. 49:3), yet in ch. 53 the Servant is not depicted as a nation but as an individual, as one who now sums up in himself the corporate experience of the whole people of Israel. Or yet again, while the figure of the Son of Man in Dan. 7:13–14 is that of an individual who is presented before God, in the same chapter the very promise that is made to the individual at v. 14 is repeated in v. 27 to Israel as a corporate entity.

We have good reason to believe, then, that the writers of the New Testament, all of whom, except for Luke, were Jews, found no difficulty in transferring Old Testament images or picture-theological expressions to the person of one individual Israelite. This one Israelite, for example, says of himself that he is Son of Man. Moreover, he implicitly accepts the role of the Servant that is depicted in Second Isaiah. Then he explicitly claims to be the true Vine. He obviously regards himself as the Shekinah, for he says: "Where two or three are gathered together in my name, there am I in the midst of them." For, traditionally, the phrase already existed in this form: "If two sit together and words of the Law are spoken between them, the Shekinah rests between them" (*Sayings of the Fathers* 3:2); and the rabbis who used this and similar expressions insisted that they did not suggest there were *shetei reshuyot,* "two divinities," in the nature of God. In fact, it was a cardinal principle of Rabbinical Judaism that Almighty God could, at will, contract himself and confine his Shekinah to be present at one small spot (cf. *Pesikta,* ed. M. Buber, p. 20a; Gen. R. 4:4). This conception of the localized presence of God earned for itself the technical term of *zimzum.* But its importance rests not in technicalities, but in its personal usage; for a Jew, loyal to his monotheistic heritage, could in all innocence exclaim: "When a man is ill, the Shekinah says, 'I feel a weariness in my head, I feel a weariness in my arm' " (T. B. San. 46a; T. B. Hag. 15b), or could regard the Shekinah as a loving, guardian angel that is present at the sickbed of an invalid (T. B. Ned. 40a). This personalizing of the Shekinah is expressed by the phrase "the Face of the Shekinah" (cf. Lev. R. 30:2), just as we have the phrase "the Face of God" at Gen. 32:30, and the words "My Face will go with you" at Ex. 33:14, and "the Angel of God's Face" at Isa. 63:9, and, with Jesus, the words "He who has seen me has seen the Father" (John 14:9).

Just as the prologue to John's Gospel is composed wholly of Hebraic terms, so too is the prologue to The Letter to the Hebrews. There Christ is spoken of as "the brightness of God's Glory" (KJV). "Brightness" is the *ziw* of the rabbis, the Splendor of God visualized in terms of light, and "glory" is the *kabod* of the Old Testament, the "tabernacling presence of God on one spot on earth." Similarly, therefore, James 2:1 can state: "Our Lord Jesus Christ, the Glory, the Shekinah." Hebrews 1:3 can say that Jesus is the *charaktēr* of God's being, the *image* of God, as the Old Latin translates the word, yet in no static, Platonic sense, for Christ upholds the universe (cf. Prov. 8:22–31 above) by the Word of power.

Again, when the Spirit descends upon him at his baptism (Matt. 3:17), Jesus "hears" from God that he is at once Israel the Son of God (Ex. 4:22; perhaps also Ps. 2:7) and Israel the Servant of God (Isa. 49:3), and that his mission is the mission of Israel, made concrete for his understanding by the appearance of the dove. The Old Testament name of "Jonah" means "dove." So with the descent of the dove upon him, Jesus "saw" his calling to be the incarnation of the Word of

God in mission to the world. (See *Ruth and Jonah,* Torch Bible Commentary, by G. A. F. Knight; The Macmillan Company, 1951).

Thus we might say that as the indwelling immanence or Shekinah of God, Jesus was the very Name of God which God has set at one spot on earth (see Matt. 1:21, for "Jesus" means "Yahweh saves"). Second Isaiah had insisted that the Lord alone is Redeemer and Savior (Isa. 43:11; 47:4). Other writers had asserted that God had placed his Name, i.e., his saving power, within the Holy of Holies in the Temple. But now both Jesus and his interpreters regard this reality as focusing upon himself (Matt. 26:61; 27:40; John 2:19–21), most particularly at the moment of his death (Matt. 27:51). So we are left with the paradox that the "place" of God's indwelling was with Israel as a whole (II Cor. 6:16; I Peter 2:5), and yet that this place was Christ.

The paradox is resolved, however, by Jesus himself. For by calling himself *the* Son, Jesus regards himself as the *one* representative "head" of the corporate Son, Israel. The Letter to the Hebrews prefers to quote the Greek version of Ps. 40 rather than the Hebrew, when it makes the point that throughout the centuries since the days of Abraham, God had been preparing a "body" for his Son Jesus (Heb. 10:5); this body is, of course, the Israel of God of old. Paul, in his turn, sees the perfect union of the corporate, empirical Israel with her Lord and God in the "one flesh" that true marriage exemplifies (Gen. 2:24; Eph. 5:23–33), in the person of Jesus Christ. In declaring that Jesus is both God and man in one, then, we can now employ the Old Testament image to interpret what we believe is fact.

In this way, then, the pictures which express reality in the Old Testament are transferred to the New. There are at least two of the great church fathers who persisted with this Hebraic pictorial thinking, and whose works are therefore of great value to us at this point. They are Irenaeus and Theodore of Mopsuestia. The former has left us at least one simple, unanalyzable, truly Biblical "picture" of the relationship between God, Christ, and the Holy Spirit. His statement, so easy to comprehend, so simple to see with the mind's eye, is that Christ and the Holy Spirit are the two arms of God. By adhering to such language, and refusing to become metaphysical and analytical, we in our turn can avoid the serious errors that Jews can so rightly point to in some of our theological expressions. It is the Jew who is right, and not we, we should remember, if we neglect the emphatic language of Isa. 43:11, "I am the Lord, and beside me there is no Savior." This we are to keep in mind even when we read in I John 4:14, for example, that "the Father sent the Son to be the Savior of the world." In earlier centuries the church played with some fantastic doctrines, in which it pitted Jesus as Savior over against God, with whom Jesus was quite at odds. When the angel of the Lord appeared to Joseph in a dream (Matt. 1:20–21), announcing the coming birth, he said: "Thou shalt call his name Jesus [Yehoshua or Yah, i.e., Jehovah, saves], for he [i.e., Yah] shall save his people from their sins." For "who can forgive sins but God alone?" (Mark 2:7). The perfect statement of this truth is made by Paul in II Cor. 5:19, where he summarizes his faith in God's redemptive activity in the words (as they are best translated), "In Christ, God was reconciling the world to himself." Note how, if we wish to be true to Hebrew thinking, it is not sufficient to declare just that "God was in Christ"; this is because God cannot be described in terms of mere being in himself. The genius of the Hebrew conception of God is to know him only as he reveals himself in loving deeds and saving acts.

The Problem of Sin, and the Sinless One. So now we approach the ontological problem that creates the gap between the faith of the Jew and the faith of the Christian. For the Jew does not understand how the Christian can believe that the God who is pure Spirit can ever really manifest his Arm, and so show himself in the form of man. Yet it is exactly the Hebraic pictorial thinking which the Jew refuses to give up that helps us most to recognize the reality of the incarnation. And here again it is Jesus' own words that help us most.

We note the paradox that Jesus never explicitly claimed divinity for himself, for that would have been an un-Godlike thing to do. We are to remember this, even as we keep in mind that he saw himself as the "David" in whom such terms as "Wonderful Counselor", "the Mighty God", "the Everlasting Father", "the Prince of Peace" (Isa. 9:6) were finally fulfilled. As Biblical scholarship has so amply made it clear, each and all of these Isaianic terms are applied, not primarily to man, but particularly to God, in other passages of the Old Testament itself. What Jesus did consistently call himself was Son of Man.

In Ezekiel the phrase occurs like a refrain. There we find that God addresses the prophet as Son of Man, in order to show him that he is a responsible being who can hear and obey God's voice. But Ezekiel is already a responsible being in this sense, for he is the spokesman of the whole People of God. Now, both Ps. 80:17 and, as we have seen, Dan., ch. 7, regard the whole People of God as "Son of Man" in this significant and far-reaching sense. For Israel has been called to be truly that corporate Man of God whom God can use for the redemption of the world. A superficial reading of Ps. 8:4, it is true, might imply that all humanity as well as individuals can be described as Son of Man. Yet we are to remember that no Psalmist would ever suppose that the God of Israel had "visited" any other nation than his own chosen people with the purpose of revealing himself in loving concern. So we are to understand that it is Israel which is Son of Man in Ps. 8 just as much as in Ps. 80.

Thus even when the writer of Gen. 1:26 declares that God created man in his own image, he was speaking as an Israelite himself, and so as a member of the Covenant People of God.

The tradition enshrined in the second and third chapter of Genesis makes crystal clear in "pictorial," symbolic language, that the original plan of God did not, however, become a fact. Man, Adam (the Hebrew word for humanity), cannot be said to be the image or the likeness or the pictorial representation of God in human flesh; for man is a fallen creature. But it is not anything inherent in his ontological nature that has induced the blurring of the image; it is man's pride and egotism that have done so. It is because he has rebelled against God's good plan for him and *only* because of this, that man, the Son of Man, and thus inevitably elect man, the People of God, is not able to show forth the Glory of God as he is called to do as God's image or as the perfect representation of the eternal God on earth.

As a matter of fact, man's rebellion has brought him to the level of the beast. Now, the pinnacle, the acme, the supreme representative head of the greatest earthly power that the world had known in Old Testament times was Nebuchadnezzar, king of Babylonia. According to Ezekiel, this monarch was hailed as "King of kings, and Lord of lords" (Ezek. 26:7). No title could possibly better describe what man can hope to be in himself. Yet this same "pinnacle" of all humanity had so far rebelled against God's plan and guidance that, in parabolic language, he is likened to a beast and not a man (Dan. 4:33). It is therefore this supreme representative Son of Man who has to eat grass like an ox and grow nails like birds' claws. That is to say, Nebuchadnezzar is not really anymore a man; he is subhuman and just a beast. *In* him, therefore, the whole of the sinful humanity whom he "represents," is in the same condition of disintegration. That is why so many harsh words are uttered by the prophets against the great powers of the earth. The nations of our sinful humanity are, in fact, often pictured as beasts, and may even be identified with the monster who inhabits the deeps of chaos under the earth. Yet the same book of Daniel that draws such pictures of man as he really is (Dan. 7:3) proceeds to declare that God will yet give the dominion, and the glory, and the kingdom forever to a Son of Man to rule (Dan. 7:14). The logic is that God could be supposed to do this thing only in the case of one who was wholly sinless, for it is only a sinless one who could possibly be his perfect instrument. In other words, the Old

Testament is aware that it is not time and space that separate God from man, nor is it flesh as against spirit, nor finitude as against infinity. It is sin, and sin alone, which forms the barrier that man cannot breast (Gen. 3:24). Whereas, where sin is absent, there is God himself in the fullness of his majesty.

Now, it is just because man is a sinner that the Old Testament forbids him to make any likeness or image of the God who has created him. For the sinner cannot imagine what the sinless can be like. But conversely, God can make an image of himself, and that was his purpose in the beginning when he created man (Gen. 1:26).

This, then, is how Jesus himself bridges the ontological gap that we have spoken of. In implicitly accepting the role of the Son of Man, Jesus was openly declaring who he believed himself to be. For he it was who said, "Which of you convinceth me of sin?" (John 8:46). It is the *sinlessness* of Jesus, therefore, which forces us to the conclusion that he is the perfect image or Face of God. It is his sinlessness, and that alone, which permits his "body" to become the very matrix of the revelation of God's Glory (John 13:31). Thus, although Jesus is "sent" from God, it is his sinlessness in his utter obedience to God as man which alone becomes the vehicle by means of which the Kingdom of God has begun to come on earth even as it is in heaven.

II. The Atonement[1]

The incarnation, however, is not the only problem to the Jewish mind. Another great difficulty is the Christian doctrine of the atonement. The point is that traditional Judaism has seen no need for any mediator, and Judaism, ever since the days of the Talmud, has declared that a Jew need only confess his sin to God in all sincerity, and God will for-

[1] This section of the chapter includes material from a paper entitled "Fundamental Differences Between Judaism and Christianity," by Frederick Neumann.

give him directly. Now, I suggest that this teaching of Judaism is a creation of the rabbinical mind. It is not, I submit, inherent in the faith of the Old Testament; far less is it to be found in the Torah that is the basis of Judaism, whether Orthodox, Conservative, or Reform. This doctrine has arisen in reaction to the Christian interpretation of the Old Testament that marked the early centuries of Christian theology, centuries when Jews and Christians were drifting apart, and growing more and more embittered against each other as the gap between them widened. The Christian believed and declared to the Hellenistic world, which included the Jews now living in Diaspora, that it could trace an unbroken line of revelation between the Old Testament cry for atonement and its fulfillment in the cross of Christ. Since, however, the Jews shared this same Old Testament with the Christian church which made this claim, the rabbis were compelled to offer a new interpretation of their common root with the church; and so in the creation of the "Rabbinical Judaism" of the early Christian centuries a break was made with the past as a form of self-defense on Jewry's part and as a declaration of the integrity of Jewish existence.

The above statement must read most provocatively to a Jew. But I make it humbly with three criteria in mind. First, these are the words of one who is aware of the often deliberate misrepresentation of Judaism that the church has exhibited in earlier centuries. Secondly, it is the statement of one who gratefully acknowledges the profoundly *positive* interpretation of the Old Testament that many Jewish writers are making now. But thirdly, it is the statement of one who seeks to make an objective, academic assessment of the facts at his command.

Both in Old Testament times and after, thoughtful Jews consistently felt the need of a mediator between Israel and Israel's God. Even in the early Christian centuries, when the controversy between the two faiths was at its height, many deeply religious minds, as we shall see, sought to concretize this need even when the rabbis warned the faithful that the Christian answer to it was false.

It is clear that the Old Testament itself regarded the existence of the priesthood and of the sacrificial system as a means of mediation between God and Israel. To that end the Israel of the Old Testament period multiplied sacrifices to the point where we today can scarcely follow what they were all about. But they were instituted and developed because of a felt need within the human heart. The prophet, too, acted in part as mediator, both as the mouthpiece of the Word, and as "interpreter," *melits,* of both Word and historical event (Isa. 43:27). We hear Abraham interceding with God for the Cities of the Plain (Gen. 18:23–33). We read of Moses actually offering himself as mediator between Israel and God in terms which show his understanding of what we would call vicarious suffering (Ex. 32:31–32). The Servant in Isa., ch. 53, whom we considered above, offered his *nephesh,* that is to say his whole being, "body, soul, and spirit," as an *'asham,* a guilt offering (Isa. 53:10) for "the many," the masses, of this world. The *principle* of mediation, therefore. is certainly present at the very heart of the Old Testament revelation. This is so even when many a passage speaks of God's mighty love and grace for the repentant sinner (cf. Isa. 1:16–20), which he is eager to bestow directly on his people.

This *principle* is continuously observable in the later literature of Israel. In Tobit 12:15 we read that the angels present to God the prayers of the saints. In the book of Enoch we meet a heavenly personality who performs the task of mediation; and even if the "Son of Man" passages are a later Christian interpolation, the original figure of Enoch himself is not. Moreover, the intercession of angels is still seen to be a central "pictorial" element. In fact, one particular angel, viz., Michael, tends to hold a unique function in this regard; and both in Enoch and in other Apocryphal literature, this office is performed in the actual presence of God in heaven. In other words, these personages represent in a pictorial manner the very nature of the living God himself, for they show that he "wrestles" within himself to the point of "repentance," or, as we would say today, to the point of having to "change his plan."

Even after the early Christian church had thought through its doctrine of Jesus as the mediator, the synagogue refused to abandon this principle of mediation. We can see how the Targums, the Aramaic versions of the Old Testament that were used as translations of the Scriptures by the Jewish community, continued to attribute to Abraham, Moses, and other figures the office of mediator with God. In fact, it sometimes even suggests their names at points where these are not mentioned in the original Hebrew text. Such is true, for example, in the Targum to The Song of Songs. We might cite to illustrate this point Targ. Cant. 1:5, for there we read of Moses going up to heaven and taking with him peace between Israel and Israel's King. At 2:15 we are told that it was the sacrifice which Abraham offered in Isaac his son that induced God not to destroy Israel for its sin with the Golden Calf. In the Targum to Zech. 12:5 the Messianic figure who is mentioned so often in the Old Testament is declared to be the Redeemer of Israel; and we should recall that this Targum found final form quite some time after the beginning of the Christian era. It is true that the redemption spoken of is from national bondage rather than from sin, but the principle is the same in both cases. In Targum Jonathan to Zech. 4:7 the Messiah is no longer a man, but is now a heavenly being.

Such a heavenly being, during the Gaonic period of Rabbinical thought, that is, between A.D. 600 and 1000, receives the name of Metatron. According to the *Jewish Encyclopedia,* VIII, 519, the word is probably a Hebraized form of the Greek *metathronos* or *metatyrannos,* that is, one who occupies the next rank to ruler. Yet this is not the only form that the *principle* of mediation takes in Jewish thought, for God's own Word, written as *Memra* in the Targums, can also be said to act as intercessor between God and Israel (Targ. Jon. to Jer. 29:14), or again in Targ. Ps.-Jon. to Num. 21:9 f.; Jer. 3:23; Isa. 45:17, where we read: "Israel has been delivered by the Word of the Lord"; or in Isa. 66:13, which runs: "As a man whom his mother comforts, so shall my

Word comfort you." Even that feminine entity, the Torah (the first five books of the Old Testament), can hold such a mediating position (cf. *Sayings of the Fathers* 2:3), so that "she" comes to maintain much the same relationship to God as that other feminine entity, Wisdom, of which we read in Prov. 8:22 ff. A good example is Exodus Rabba 29, for it employs typical Hebraic picture language in saying that Torah stands before the Holy One and intercedes for Israel.

When the Christian hears of Jewish ideas such as these, he must not ridicule them on the ground that they are "non-theological." Nor should he expect to find a theology of mediation built upon such elusive material. He should, rather, regard these pictures as fleeting representations of what the Jew, being a son of the Old Testament revelation, knows in his heart is a necessary *principle* because of the nature of the living God. But ever since the rise of the New Testament the Jew has not dared to formulate a doctrine of mediation. This is because, were he to do so, he would have to premise that the Jewish Jesus was the only ultimate "picture" of mediation that he could wholeheartedly use, for only Jesus fulfills all the requirements of one who is to mediate completely between God and man.

Isaiah, Chapter 53, in the Targums. The Jew's overt rejection of the Christian interpretation of the Old Testament is nowhere better seen than in the deliberate mistranslation of parts of the fourth Servant Song in Isa., chs. 52 and 53, that we find in the Targum Jonathan. The reader will notice that the total meaning of the poem has here been transformed to mean something quite different from what the original Hebrew is saying:

52:14 As the house of Israel looked to him during many days, because their countenance was darkened among the peoples, and their complexion beyond the sons of men. . . .

53:2 The righteous will grow up before him like blooming shoots, and like a tree which sends forth its roots to streams of water will they increase—a holy generation in the land that was in need of him: his countenance will be no profane countenance, and the terror at him will not be the terror at an ordinary man. . . .

53:3 . . . he will cut off the glory of all the kingdoms; they will be prostrate and mourning. . . .

53:5 . . . by his instruction peace shall be increased upon us, and by our devotion to his words our sins will be forgiven us.

53:7 . . . the mighty ones of the peoples he will deliver up like a lamb to the slaughter. . . . There shall be none before him opening his mouth or saying a word. . . .

53:8 . . . he will cause the dominion of the Gentiles to pass away from the land of Israel, and transfer to them the sins which my people have committed.

53:10 . . . it is the Lord's good pleasure to refine and purify the remnant of his people, so as to cleanse their souls from sin: these shall look upon the kingdom of their Messiah, their sons and their daughters shall be multiplied, they shall prolong their days, and those who perform the Law of the Lord shall prosper in his good pleasure.

53:11 From the subjection of the nations he will deliver their souls, they shall look upon the punishment of those that hate them. . . . By his wisdom he will hold the guiltless free from guilt, in order to bring many into subjection to the Law; and for their sins he will intercede. . . .

Many rabbis rejected this paraphrase of the Servant Song, though it was the translation commonly used. Yet the great Rashi adhered to its essential point of view. It is a relief, therefore, to turn to faithful attempts at its translation and interpretation by such scholars as Sa'adyah Gaon, or David Qimḥi. Many Rabbinical scholars prefer to suggest that the chapter refers to the Messiah yet to come; so Yapheth ben Ali and Mosheh ben Naḥman, Abraham ibn Ezra, Jacob ben Reuben the Rabbanite, and others, who all wrestled with the chapter in polemic against the church's understanding of it; and this state of things continued right on into the Middle Ages.

The Question of Taking Sin Seriously. The rebellion by Rabbinical Judaism that we note here against the plain words of this section of the Old Testament has induced modern Judaism to align itself with the pagan world at large in not taking sin seriously. On the ground, therefore, that it does not take sin seriously, Judaism now sees no need for a Mediator between God and man, nor does it understand the drastic redemptive action that God has effected through the cross of Christ. The synagogue has broken with the plainly worded view of the nature of man that every strand of the Old Testament makes explicit. For example, along with modern educated agnostic man, Judaism does not agree with the words of Genesis, "And God saw that the wickedness of man was great in the earth, and that every imagination of the thoughts of his heart was only evil continually" (Gen. 6:5), a reality that persists even after the curse on the earth is removed (Gen. 8:21); nor does Judaism now stand beside Isaiah as he became aware of his total sinfulness when he found himself in the presence of the all-holy God. For Judaism does not appreciate Isaiah's reaction to that experience when he cried: "Woe is me, for I am undone [actually, "reduced to negation"]; because I am a man of unclean lips, and I dwell in the midst of a people of unclean lips" (Isa. 6:5). Therefore, Judaism cannot enter into the experience of Peter who, when he suddenly discovered that the Jesus of Nazareth whom he knew personally so well was none other than the Arm of the Lord *revealed* (cf. Isa. 53:1), exclaimed, "Depart from me, for I am a sinful man, O Lord" (Luke 5:8). The Christian should be aware, however, that Reform Judaism is now diverging from Orthodox Judaism on this issue, and is reassessing the content of a phrase that is characteristic of Judaism, viz., *Simḥat Torah,* rejoicing in the Torah.

This inability to recognize the evil in this world as something monstrous, or rather, as the Bible would prefer to say, Satanic, Dr. Bruno Bettelheim, at the Eighth Annual Rosenwald Lecture, December, 1962, has called "the ghetto mentality" in the Jews. This inability to recognize the power of evil, as I have said, is something that Jewry shares with paganism. In recent times we have seen great numbers of Jewish people refusing to accept the possibility that Hitler really meant what he said, when he announced in advance the extermination of the Jews as his program, even while those very same Jews had already heard how Lenin had exterminated several million of his foes. The Jewish faith is still optimistic about human nature despite every reason not to be. The word "imagination," *yetser,* which we found in Gen. 6:5, today means "tendency" in Jewish thought. But it declares, what Genesis does not do, that there are two *yetsers* in the human heart. Thus, while the one is indeed a tendency toward the evil, the other is clearly toward the good.

Then again, as a result of its prime insistence on the Torah (the first five books of the Old Testament) as the Word of God, traditional Judaism has relegated the Prophets to second place. Therefore it has paid scant attention to the serious view of sin exhibited by all the prophets. In fact, the plain statement of Amos that since Israel has been specially chosen, therefore Israel is particularly under judgment (Amos 3:1–2) has remained an enigma until recent times. It is only now, as Jewish scholars read the Biblical theology which has been developed by the Christian church, that Judaism has been forced to look at itself afresh. (See, for example, Abraham J. Heschel's justly acclaimed volume *The Prophets of Israel.*)

Hosea likened the sin of Israel to the rottenness you can find in the heart of an apple (Hos. 5:12). Isaiah declared that Israel's sin was so far-reaching that Israel could no longer be called the People of God, for she had virtually turned herself into Sodom and Gomorrah (Isa. 1:10). The Second Isaiah speaks of his own people as nothing better than a worm and a louse (Isa. 41:14, where "men" should probably be read as "louse" in parallel with "worm"). Yet it is *this* people with whom God has entered into covenant fellowship "forever," "no matter what," as we might say today. In the light of

Hosea's interpretation of the covenant made at Sinai as a virtual marriage between God and Israel, we might also render the word *ḥesed,* the steadfast love which forms the bond of that marriage covenant, in a modern way by the phrase "the love that will not let me go."

The Judgment of God. This wholly trustworthy and faithful love of God finds itself confronted, in the days of the prophets, by an intolerable position. The point is this: True to its Hebraic expression of reality, the Old Testament can speak of sin only in a secondary manner. This is because sin is only an abstraction. Apart from people who sin, there can not be any such thing as sin. This awareness of the personal nature of sin suggests to the prophets that its roots lie not so much in the breaking of God's law as in the disruption of personal relationships. This is seen when Israel gives her loyalty, not to her divine Husband, but to the Baals who are the gods of her Canaanite neighbors. And so the prophets speak of sin in terms of apostasy, and of "going awhoring after other gods." Since, then, it is not *sin* so much as *sinners* that God has now to deal with, the righteous judgment of Israel's God rests not upon her sins but upon Israel herself. That is why God must necessarily declare: "So I will be to them like a lion, like a leopard I will lurk beside the way. . . . I will fall upon their breast, and there I will devour them like a lion, as a wild beast would rend them" (Hos. 13:8). Such divine action Martin Luther has called God's "strange work," his *opus alienum,* a direct translation of Isaiah's words at ch. 28:21. Consequently, God may have to force his people into a position in which they must finally realize that of themselves they are nothing, that they are indeed a worm, that their own goodness is as short-lived as the morning dew (Hos. 6:4), till they become really aware that "we are all as an unclean thing, and all our righteousnesses are as filthy rags" (Isa. 64:6; cf. Zech. 3:3–4). Thus God may need to "make the heart of this people fat, and make their ears heavy, and shut their eyes; lest they see with their eyes, and hear with their ears, and understand with their heart, and convert, and be healed" (Isa. 6:10), the message which Isaiah was given to proclaim once he had recognized how utterly sinful were both he and his people. The point is that should Israel return to God in contrition, her confession then could only produce a "slight healing," to use Jeremiah's words (Jer. 6:14; 8:11). And a slight healing is of no use to a rotten apple. That is why the prophets see the action of God in destroying Jerusalem in 586 B.C. as "putting Israel to death." For that is what happened in Ezekiel's view when "My servant Nebuchadnezzar" (Jer. 25:9) wiped the state of Judah off the map.

One of the earliest statements of faith in the whole Old Testament is the so-called Song of Moses in Deut., ch. 32. Yet even in the tenth century B.C., where Professor Albright would place this poem, it was recognized of the Lord that "I, even I, am He, and there is no god like Me: I kill, and I make alive; I wound and I heal" (v. 39).

This, then, is the essential insight into the sinfulness of sin that traditional Judaism has lost. Since the cross of Christ has focused upon itself the full significance of those words of Deut., ch. 32, in sheer contrariness of mind Judaism, in the early Christian centuries, chose to expunge their content from its faith. The Rabbinical leaders of Israel have since declared that while of course all mankind are sinful, any man may receive the forgiveness of God merely for the asking, provided that in asking he is truly sincere. In other words, Judaism has forsaken its own Hebraic roots, and has become more Hellenized than it cares to acknowledge. For it is the "Platonist" who would seek forgiveness for those abstractions we call sins. It is only the "Hebraist" who beats his breast in self-despair, and cries: "God, forgive *me* [not, "my sins"] for *I* am a *sinner*."

It is the Old Testament which taught the world that God must deal, not with sins, but with the sinner. Thus it is the Old Testament which has naturally identified the abstraction that we call forgiveness with the experience of being born again (Ezek., ch. 37). "Except a corn of wheat fall into the ground and die, it abideth alone: but if it die, it bringeth forth much fruit." (John 12:24.) It is just this truth, then, that through fear of identifying itself with the Christian church, the synagogue has resolutely refused to admit. It is the truth that man, even covenant Israelite man, is so evil that he does not know even what it means to repent or how to begin to do so. We recall the words of the poet Robert Burns:

> O wad some power the giftie gie us
> To see oursels as others see us!

Burns knew that he could not properly confess his sins, simply because he did not sufficiently see into himself to discover what his sins really were. All that a man can in fact recognize are some of his sins; he cannot however recognize his *sin*. Thus forgiveness cannot depend upon confession, or man is in a sorry plight. This plight of his is rendered doubly serious if, in fact, he is in a state of rebellion which makes him incapable of confessing those sins which even he might be expected to recognize. In other words, although repentance is beyond human capacity, the synagogue prays every day in the *Tefillah* (Amidah):

> Our Father, bring us back to Your Torah;
> Our King, draw us near to Your service;
> Lead us back, truly repentant before You.
> Praised are You, O Lord, who welcomes repentance.

So we see how right Isaiah was to declare that it is actually of the goodness of God that he hardens our heart. For he must bring us to the point where we are forced to admit that he has destroyed "our Jerusalem," so that we are really living in exile. Professor Floreen, who contributes Chapter 6 to this volume, has said: "The Jews are that people which refuses to die." And so the Jews are that people which misses the possibility that is granted to the seed that falls into the ground. They miss the possibility of being born again and so of being raised to a new dimension of life. They do not know what it is to taste the life of the risen Christ, which is the life of "the world to come," the *'olam ha-ba'*. For they have not been able to confess that Christ has done for them something that no one but God ought to be able to do, viz., descend after them into "that life of death" where they had been spending their days in rebellion against God, and then as *Mediator,* as *Intermediary,* as *Redeemer,* as *Savior,* restore them to where they belong in the purpose of God, viz., in their Father's home. The Christian, then, does not just experience the forgiveness of his sins. Rather, in and through the death and resurrection of him who is both God and man in one, the Christian is raised out of the death of his exile into that fullness of life which is fellowship with God and which the New Testament describes as the new life of the Kingdom of Heaven. And this life is wonderfully, bewilderingly *new,* for it is the gift of God from "the other side."

On the other hand, both of us, Jews and Christians together, are faced with a strange reality. It is that despite God's forgiveness in which we both share, sin is still very much with us, and the world is not yet redeemed. That this is so constitutes an old and ever-repeated Jewish argument against the Christian faith. War and strife, racial and economic oppression, Jews point out, still desecrate God's creation despite the cross of Christ. People continue to sin as if nothing had happened two thousand years ago. And the Christian's sinning is not more but rather definitely less excusable than the Jew's sinning. Furthermore, the Old and New Testaments both promise a cosmic redemption (e.g., Isa. 11:6–11; Hab. 2:14; Rom. 8:18–25; Eph. 1:9–10). Nothing of it has materialized as yet. Where is then the promised Kingdom? What about Christ's promise to bring in the Kingdom?

The answer to this widely held objection obviously requires a clean break with Christian self-righteousness. Israel is the paradigmatic people. Israel is the divine pattern for the revelation of God's ways with men. The proper typological understanding of the Old Testament sees in the history of the church the same judgments that Israel's prophets pronounced upon their own people. It would be an intolerable presumption on the part of the church to claim that the prophets' uncompromising message of death to which we referred above was aimed only at the Israel of old, and not at the church itself as well. The horrid pretension on the part of Christians of being "better" than the Jewish people involves the forfeiture of the Christians' standing as God's children. When we hear the words, "The Lord has a controversy with his people," we should know that they refer to Jews and Christians alike (Hos. 4:1; Micah 6:2). For this we have the explicit word in the New Testament, "The time has come for judgment to begin with the household of God" (I Peter 4:17).

What, then, is the advantage of the church? It is that Christians are privileged to hallow the Name of God, who has a controversy with his people, by means of being God's active witnesses against their very selves. Throughout this age in which we now live, however, the hallowing of the Name by Christians can be regarded only as incipient. Figuratively speaking, the history of God's people is like the assembling of a large orchestra against the Day when the divine Conductor will direct it in public. Till then it is our duty to tune our instruments, to practice diligently, and to invite our prospective fellow musicians to join us. The orchestra can only start performing the eternal symphony of the love of God once all members needed to play the score have gathered. Then the Son of God will raise his baton.

As it seeks to rejudaize its Christology today, then, the church is rediscovering more than one ancient Hebraic conception. With the return to Biblical theology that is characteristic of our generation, it is gaining a new understanding of the essential unity, for example, of matter and spirit, of soul and body, of time and eternity, in fact, of the unity of all things within the unity of the one God who has made them all. This "rejudaissance" of Christian theology that is going on today may well be leading the church, under God, to a much closer understanding of the essential Jewish categories of thought which it has neglected in the past; and at the same time, it may well be leading the synagogue to a clearer understanding of the essentially Hebraic theology which the church once employed to express its faith. Please God the gap between the church and the synagogue may be greatly lessened by the consecrated work of Biblical scholars from within the two strands that together comprise the one Israel of God.

Chapter Eight

THE ONE ISRAEL OF GOD

James R. Brown, professor at Nashotah House, Nashotah, Wisconsin, where he is preparing students for the Episcopal ministry, possesses a unique advantage over most Christian ministers. For he studied for three years in Hebrew Union College, Cincinnati, as an Interfaith Fellow. His chapter will be of special interest to Christians who have not attempted to keep up-to-date with American Jewish thinking. Judaism, in its three branches, is passing through profound changes today. Some of these philosophical movements are reflected in the works of Jewish thinkers about whom the Christian ought to be aware. Protestant Christianity is rethinking itself today in secular society. It is also rethinking itself in relation to Roman Catholicism. Why should it not rethink itself also in its relationship to Judaism, even as Judaism is doing in its relationship to the Christian world?

—*The Editor*

The Jewish people are living alongside of us Christians in the cities of North America. Their prophetic interpretation of the Old Testament (see Chapter 3) is not the same as ours, though this is an area of study where we have begun to draw closer together (see Chapter 10). They have their Messianic hopes, as we have ours (see Chapter 4). Their presence among us, however, is a "mystery" (see Chapter 2). The Jewish people claim, and of course rightly, that they are Israel, the ancient People of God. But, then, we too claim, and we too believe rightly, that we are Israel. For we claim, along with the Gentile Corinthians to whom Paul was writing, that "all our fathers were . . . baptized unto Moses" (I Cor. 10:1–2). For along with the Jewish people we accept the Old Testament as our Scripture, and Abraham, Isaac, and Jacob as our ancestors. Yet for us the prophetic hope was finally actualized, and became once for all "yea and amen" in Jesus Christ. How, then, can we be the one Israel of God, Jews and Christians together?

I. The Book of Israel

We may put it this way: the Bible begins by showing us how mankind, created by God for life and fellowship with himself, has misused its gift of free will to choose instead the way of sin and death. What has God done about it? We see the divine plan of redemption taking shape in the call of an obedient man of faith, Abraham, to be the head of a community through which the whole world is to be blessed, a community united in holiness and love. Then the main story gets under way, and Israel becomes the People of God in virtue of the mighty acts whereby he delivered them from bondage, entered into a covenant with them, gave them his law, and established them in their own land. All this is of grace alone; there is no thought of any merit or virtue on Israel's part as a result of which she is chosen. But the nation has to learn what it means and how much it costs to be the People of God; and in the rest of the Old Testament we read of its struggles as it passes through the fires of judgment and disaster. Gradually a forward-looking hope emerges, patterned after the events of the old deliverance; there would be a greater exodus from a bondage to that of which the bondage to Egypt was but a parable, viz., bondage to sin and death; there would be a covenant written on the heart; there would be the gift of the Spirit, a renewed people under a greater David; nor would these blessings be for Israel alone, but all nations would share in them.

The New Testament simply says that this supreme crisis has taken place through him who was victorious in his sacrifice over sin and death. The promised outpouring of the Spirit has happened; the meaning of the crisis is that God has visited and redeemed his people so that its doors stand open to people of all nations, and Jew and Gentile alike dwell therein, "Abraham's seed, heirs according to the Promise." Thus the Bible *as a whole,* the Christian believes, is the Book of Israel, and God's Word to Israel. Thus we need to take care that we do not talk loosely as though we Gentiles had replaced the Jews in the purpose of God, and as though the latter were henceforth consigned to perdition. What the Bible teaches us is that we who are not Jews have entered upon a heritage which God has prepared for us by his dealings with the Jewish people, a heritage of restored fellowship with himself, one that is in fact incomplete if we do not share it with them. There are not two peoples of God, but one, and the "church" is by Pauline definition the place where Gentile meets Jew and the two are made one (Eph. 1:11–22). If this does not happen, if Christians do not engage in this confrontation, can there be said to be a church?

This is the spiritual fact. The historical fact has been, of course, that Christendom has often shown a marked ambiguity with respect to its Jewish heritage. On the one hand, it has treasured that heritage for obvious reasons. Jesus himself was a Jew, of Jewish lineage and descent; so also was his mother; and it was to his own people that his mission was, in the first place, directed. The first disciples also were Jews, and when in the course of a single generation Christianity passed over into the Greek world, it was only a stubborn insistence on the *Hebraic* elements in the gospel that prevented our faith, humanly speaking, from disintegrating into yet another form of religiosity. These elements were the ardent, instinctive monotheism of the Old Testament, its belief in God as personal, holy, and creator, whose acts history reveals as he works within it for the salvation of his creation. All these became embodied in corporate, essentially *Jewish* forms of worship. On the other hand, however, there is the long record of suffering inflicted on the Jewish people by the church in the name of Christ, so that the cross, which to us is the symbol of life and peace, has become in fact to the Jew the symbol of persecution and death.

II. A Renewed Concern with Judaism

There are, however, many signs today among Christians of a reawakened spiritual sympathy with Jewish traditions and faith. That is why this volume is being published now. The long history of hatred and persecution of the Jews culminated in Nazi Germany in our own day: six million Jews perished, one out of every three in the world at that time, one and one half million of them children. The holocaust was carried through by a people reared for centuries in the Christian tradition. Why did it happen? Could it have happened at all if there had been a genuinely Christian climate of opinion about the Jews? How had the church failed to speak the word of reconciliation here?

Then in 1948 we witnessed the emergence of the modern state of Israel: the ram's horn was sounded in the great synagogue of Tel Aviv and the exile was over. No Jew need live in Galuth (exile) any longer. The return, as Bishop Neill noted, has "brought home the Jewish problem to innumerable Christians with new force" (*The Church and the Jewish People,* edited by Göte Hedenquist, p. 18).

But there is a further development, one that is bound to have a powerful effect in the long run upon the attitude of Christianity to Jews and Judaism, and that is the reawakened preoccupation with the Jewish heritage of Christianity on the part of Biblical scholars and the fact that theology once again means *Biblical* theology. Time was, not so long ago, when much critical work on the New Testament tended to stress the Hellenistic background of our faith—the Greek mystery religions, the idea of the dying god, and so on. More recent study, however, finds that the influence of Hellenism was, in fact, peripheral; instead, we have come to realize the extent to which Judaism was the real matrix of Christian institutions and of the thought forms that these presuppose. At the same time, in the field of Old Testament studies, the older "evolutionary" school viewed the Old Testament not so much as the story of the revelation of God to Israel, but as the story of how Israel moved from (it was held) the virtual superstition of patriarchal days to the lofty monotheism of the great prophets, and how it developed from the expression of narrowly particularist ideas of a chosen people to a broad universalism and to a religion for all mankind. This view tended to make the Old Testament simply an interesting, but rather remote, example of the development of higher and nobler ideas about God as they have been given to us by a nation that had, as the saying went, "a genius for religion." Thus the Old Testament was not much more relevant for Christians than, say, the Buddhist scriptures.

But what if, in the Bible, God is not Object but Subject? In many ways the disturbed and distracted period in which we live has affinities with that of the Bible. The classic Biblical themes of the transcendence of God, of God as the Lord and Judge of history, and of man as created for the freedom of grace yet knowing also the captivity of sin—these things have come alive for us with an intensity of meaning which perhaps would not have been possible in the more static political and philosophical climate of a couple of generations ago, the period when the old approach took shape. More recent studies realize also that the old approach owed more to the Hegelian philosophy of history than to the unbiased reading of the Old Testament itself, and are trying to interpret the Bible from within, even as it is viewed by those who shared its faith and hope. We see that the Bible is primarily about a movement of God to man, and only secondarily about a movement of man to God. This means that the Old Testament must be regarded not as the record of how a somewhat distant ancient people advanced from lower to higher theological conceptions, so that it is, in effect, just one religious classic among many, but rather, as the story of how God worked out his saving purpose in history.

III. The Ecumenical Movement and Judaism

There are signs, then, of a renewed Christian sympathy with Jewish traditions and faith; so it was natural that this should find some expression in the ecumenical movement. At the First Assembly of the World Council of Churches at Amsterdam in 1948 a report on "The Christian Approach to the Jews" was formally received and passed on to the member churches for their serious consideration, together with a number of recommendations. In it there was frank confession of Christian guilt with respect to the Jewish people, a recognition that time and time again we have failed in charity, and that we have helped to foster an image of the Jews which has contributed to anti-Semitism—a "sin against God and man," as the Report bluntly reminds us. Again, the Report recognized that we have all too often left the task of the proclamation of the Christian gospel among the Jews to special agencies within our communions. Against this it stated that "our churches must consider the responsibility for missions to the Jews as a normal part of parish work." And the Report had a section on "The Special Meaning of the Jewish People for Christian Faith," in which it affirmed that "in the design of God, Israel has a unique position. . . . By the history of Israel God prepared the manger in which in the fullness of time He put the Redeemer of all mankind."

There is much in this Report that is well said and for which we cannot be too grateful. But it seems fair to say also that the writers of the Report saw our approach to the Jews as simply an aspect of the Lord's general missionary commission: "Go ye into all the world and preach the Gospel to every creature." "The fulfillment of this commission," it said, "requires that we *include* the Jewish people in our evangelistic task."

But here it is that difficulties arise. Can we, in fact, think of the issue in quite this way? With the Bible before us, can we simply put the Jewish people on the same level as all others? The Biblical pattern of mission is "First the Jew, *and also* the Gentile." Here in the Report it is inverted: it becomes a mission to the Gentile and, together with him, the Jew. In the Bible, further, the Jewish people has a unique position ("unique," let us note, does not mean "privileged"), for it is in a covenant of election, and so is itself entrusted with a mission. Paul speaks of a Jewish "advantage" (see Chapter 5) and of Israel as "the holy root" (Rom. 3:1; 11:16). Would not a Judaism true to itself rightly reject such an approach as the Report envisaged?

The Second Assembly, Evanston, U.S.A. At the Second Assembly, held in Evanston in 1954, our topic produced some of the most spirited debates of the whole meeting. An advisory committee of theologians had prepared a report on the Main Theme, "Christ—The Hope of the World." But it soon became clear that many delegates thought the report seriously deficient in the matter of the evangelization of the Jews. No one was denying either the place of old Israel or the Jewish roots of Christianity. "The issue was," wrote W. E. Garrison in *The Christian Century* for September 29, 1954, "as to whether Scripture (especially Rom., chs. 9 to 11) proves such an indissoluble relation between Judaism and Christianity that those who, on the basis of other texts, have a lively hope of the second coming of Christ when certain conditions have been fulfilled, must have a special concern for the conversion of the Jews; or, whether, on the other hand, 'there is no difference between the Jew and the Greek' (Rom. 10:12), and at the present stage in the world's history the church should have an equal concern for the conversion of Hindus, Muslims, Jews, Africans, and all other peoples." A paragraph along the lines indicated in the first half of this quotation was, in fact, inserted in the report, but a movement to delete it won the day by 195 votes to 150. The main supporters of the paragraph were European, and some of them well-known helpers of the Jews during Hitler's persecution. We may doubt whether all of them were prepared to subscribe to so prosaic an interpretation of Rom., chs. 9 to 11, as would appear, but their vote indicated a serious concern for the special place that Scripture as a whole attaches to the Jews. Opposition arose in part out of the emergence upon the scene of the modern state of Israel, and the thought that references to Israel might carry embarrassing political overtones, and might also handicap the work of the churches in the Middle East. Against this, Lutheran Bishop Hans Lilje, of Germany, pointed out that the references in the report were obviously to ancient Israel, or to Israel dispersed, not to the modern state. In any case, he observed, "the Assembly would have to face up to the New Testament evidence and not retreat from any political implications involved."

Another line of opposition appeared in the speech of a distinguished lay delegate of the Protestant Episcopal Church who "objected strongly to the reference to the Jews. Insisting that his views had no political implication, he said the reference would make for bad interfaith relations and would harm rather than help any valid evangelistic intention" (*The Christian Century,* September 8, 1954). The next year, in his *Protestant—Catholic—Jew: An Essay in American Religious Sociology* (p. 261), Will Herberg noted, "In Europe an omission of such a reference to the Jews would very likely have been regarded as an outcropping of anti-semitic prejudice, reminiscent of the Nazi exclusion of the Jews from the scope of the Church; in the United States, to include such reference was felt even by earnest Christians to be somehow insulting to the Jews and an impairment of 'interfaith relations.' "

The matter was not done with at Evanston, however, despite the adverse vote. The Assembly decided to pass this issue on to its member churches "for further study and ecumenical conversations," and Dr. Joseph Sittler, of Chicago, presented a statement signed by two dozen determined delegates; it is printed in Appendix 6 of *The Evanston Report:* "Statement on the Hope of Israel." Here it is said: "Our concern in this issue is wholly biblical and is not to be confused with any political attitude towards the State of Israel. We believe that Jesus Christ is the Saviour of all mankind. In Him there is neither Jew nor Greek, but we also believe that God elected Israel for the carrying out of His saving purpose. . . . Whether we are scandalized or not, that means that we are grafted into the old tree of Israel (Rom. 11:24), so that the People of the New Covenant cannot be separated from the People of the Old Covenant. The New Testament, however, speaks also of the 'fulness' of Israel, when God will manifest His glory by bringing back His 'eldest son' into the one fold of His grace (Rom. 11:12–36; Matt. 23:29). This belief is an indispensable element of our one united hope for Jew and Gentile in Jesus Christ. . . . To expect Jesus Christ means to hope for the conversion of the Jewish people, and to love Him means to love the people of God's promise. . . . We cannot be one in Christ nor can we truly believe and witness to the promise of God if we do not recognize that it is still valid for the people of the promise made to Abraham."

New Delhi, 1961. The third Assembly was held at New Delhi in 1961. It has often been pointed out that the ecumenical movement was short of a sizable part of Christendom in the shape of the Roman Catholic Church, and for the first time delegates from that communion now attended, as observers, a World Council Assembly. But as an editorial in *The Christian Century* pointed out (January 3, 1962), "Overlooked or ignored was the possibility of having at New Delhi an observer from the mother religion, Judaism." The theme of the Assembly was "Jesus Christ the Light of the World," and it issued (or rather, reissued, for it harked back to Amsterdam) a resolution denouncing anti-Semitism; a Jewish member of the press is credited with having saved the Assembly from some unfortunate wording at the end of the resolution.

The issue raised at Evanston was again heard. The resolution read in part: "In Christian teaching the historic events which led to the Crucifixion should not be so presented as to foster upon the Jewish people of today responsibilities which belong to our corporate humanity and not to one race or community. Jews were the first to accept Jesus and Jews are not the only ones who do not yet recognize him." Dr. Schnyder, of the Swiss Protestant Church Federation, proposed "that the last but one sentence of the draft Resolution should be ended at the words 'corporate humanity' and this new sentence inserted to follow: 'On the contrary, the Jews remain God's chosen people (cf. Rom., chs. 9 to 11), for even their rejection for a time must contribute to the world's salvation.' " The Report continues:

> Dr. Visser 't Hooft said that those who had worked on this resolution had been very much aware of the previous discussions within the WCC, especially at the Evanston Assembly. The basic theological problem referred to by previous speakers was one on which there was as yet no consensus of opinion. An attempt to speak on this aspect of the matter could only result in the kind of divided counsels which were so much in evidence at Evanston. On the other hand if the Assembly would content itself with a simple statement directed to the practical issue of anti-semitism it would be possible to reach complete agreement. . . . The Chairman asked Dr. Mackie if the Policy Reference Committee had discussed the theological questions raised by Dr. Schnyder's proposal. Dr. Mackie answered that it had not done so.[1]

IV. The One Israel

It would seem that here is a topic which should indeed be an urgent concern of the ecumenical movement. There is a common life, a unity that God has created and made, in and by the death and resurrection of his Son. Christians of all communions are today concerned with the implementation of that unity, but can we legitimately reduce our en-

[1] *The New Delhi Report,* edited by W. A. Visser 't Hooft (Association Press, 1962), pp. 148–150. Dr. Schnyder withdrew his proposal with the assurance that it would be referred to in the minutes of the Assembly.

deavors to what is in fact a Catholic-Protestant dialogue? There is the broader issue of Jewish-Christian confrontation. I am thinking here of a valuable book called *Martin Buber and Christianity: A Dialogue Between Israel and the Church,* by Father Hans Urs Von Balthasar, the Swiss Roman Catholic theologian. He points out that schism involves impoverishment, and not only on one side. He draws attention on page 99 to some words of Paul Démann: "The rift between the Church of the nations and an isolated Israel resulted in the Church becoming to a certain extent *déraciné.* Very soon it found itself dangerously, though not of course entirely, cut off from its roots, estranged from the biblical fatherland of its forbears, and from an innate semitic way of thought, from the human soil in which the word of God was incarnate, and in which, finally, the Logos himself became flesh. . . . The Church had therefore to become incarnate in other peoples and cultures, those of the Hellenistic world . . . and that involved great dangers. . . . This becomes obvious when it is a matter of translating the real living substance of the Church's message." (See Chapter 7 of this volume.)

There is a real sense, then, in which we can think of the Jewish-Christian separation as the first schism, and it involved no ordinary loss. Father Démann would hold that it is at the root of all subsequent schisms in Christian unity, above all, that between the East and West, and that of the sixteenth century, for "Luther (with inadequate means) turned back to the semitic values and thought forms which had been lost or not fully incorporated in the western tradition, and attempted to defend their right as against a Greek and philosophical type of theology." There are two further points that follow from this line of thought: (*a*) We speak of an approach to the Jews, when we are in fact thinking of an approach to *individual* Jews. But what of the people as a whole? Father Démann says that it is pointless to regard Israel and the church as two separate and distinct peoples of God, for the Bible knows only one. The church is indeed the final Israel and is "the fullness of Christ" requiring no completion, but on the level of history this has yet to be realized. It would be legitimate in a sense to speak of the Gentile church and of the Jewish people as "complementary," and our present recovery of Old Testament theology and spirituality shows that such is not an empty term. "Individual conversions may be very fruitful; but the whole meaning and sense of the continued existence of Israel simply cannot be that Israel should be absorbed into the Church by multiplying them. Israel has a destiny as a people. And once Christians have opened their eyes to that fact, they then will not merely think of the individual Jews in Israel, but think in terms of a better understanding and convergence between the two separated halves of the people of God." (*b*) If the term "mission" is looked at like this, we may wonder whether it is being rightly used with regard to the Jewish people. In the Bible it is the Jews who have the "mission"—for they are to be a "light to lighten the Gentiles" and are to bring the Gentiles to Israel's Messiah. Is the work of the church not more precisely seen less as a "mission" *to* Israel than as a call to it to be faithful to its own divinely given vocation?

The discussions at Evanston in particular, then, revealed the uncertainty of the church in North America in the matter of the right approach to the Jews, an uncertainty that is still with us and that results in frustration of thought and action.

It rests in part in our not understanding what Judaism is. The Jew similarly is not clear as to what the church stands for. (See Chapter 10.) There is the fragmentation of Christendom and the variety of Christian belief. But in any case Jewish experience of the church in modern times has been diverse. Many have memories of the Orthodox Church, of which Arthur Hertzberg has written: "So long as the Tsar was in power in Russia, under the influence of a reactionary Church there was organized persecution of the Jews." Others have been approached by militant revivalist groups and think of the church solely in terms of these, and of a naïve use of Messianic prophecy. Or again, since the Jew does not accept the historic Christian claims for Christ, it is perhaps natural that he should look with favor on minimizing studies of the Gospels along rather commonplace ethical lines or those which regard Paul as in effect the true author of a somewhat morose Christianity. But the old "liberal Protestant" era is over, and the Jew is not helped to communicate with the Christian if he regards its utterance as the last word in Biblical scholarship.

In 1958, in his *Pious and Secular America* (Charles Scribner's Sons), the distinguished theologian Reinhold Niebuhr published an essay on Christians and Jews in Western civilization. It is almost an impertinence to say it, but the essay is full of the good things we have come to expect from the author; not the least of them is the way in which it brings out the things Christians and Jews have in common and how there is a line on one side of which there stand together the people of Israel and the church which knows and acknowledges the God of Abraham, Isaac, and Jacob, and God's mighty acts within history, and on the other, those who do not. This unity of church and Israel is what creates a contrast with all other religions. But Niebuhr then goes on to state that our missionary activities among the Jews are wrong, "not only because they are futile and have little fruit to boast for their exertions. They are wrong because the two faiths despite differences are sufficiently alike for the Jew to find God more easily in terms of his own religious heritage than by subjecting himself to the hazards of guilt feeling involved in a conversion to a faith, which, whatever its excellencies, must appear to him as a symbol of an oppressive majority culture."

There is here a clear recognition that conversion is not simply an intellectual process. The Jew, even the secular Jew, is the member of a people with a history. What that history has often been is indicated by the fact that Orthodox Eastern Jews call baptism *shmad,* a term that means both apostasy and betrayal of Judaism. Dr. Niebuhr, in fact, goes on to say, "Practically nothing can purify the symbol of Christ as the image of God in the imagination of the Jew from the taint with which ages of Christian oppression in the name of Christ tainted it."

Niebuhr's view is somewhat similar to that of Franz Rosenzweig, which is that Christianity and Judaism are two religions with a single center, both worshiping the same God. Judaism is for the Jews; Christianity, the "daughter religion," is for the Gentiles. Yet a Christian can hold such a view only if Christology is relegated to a secondary place. For it makes nothing of the unity of the two Testaments, of Christ's claim to fulfill the law, of our Lord as the Second Adam, the head of the human race, in whom mankind (and thus not only the Gentiles) makes a fresh beginning; and finally, it makes nothing of the assertion that God *has* visited and redeemed his people, and that there *is* a unity of Jew and Gentile in the world, with Christ its substance.

It is not surprising, then, that both Christians and Jews in their mutual confusion should take refuge in interfaith cooperation. There is, of course, need of this and there is plenty of room for it at various levels of our civic life. However, it is when interfaith cooperation is accompanied by the view that religion is like one and the same cake with three possible kinds of frosting—Catholic, Protestant, and Jewish—according to taste, and that controversial discussion or missionary zeal is undesirable and even an invasion of another's privacy that both Christians and Jews will dissent. One recalls the argument used at Evanston for the deletion of a reference to any Christian witness to Jews: "It would make for bad interfaith relations."

The final issue we may raise here is that despite a unity on many things, there is in fact a great wall of separation between the Jewish people and Christianity. The average churchgoer is unaware of it, simply because he does not know the long history of persecution inflicted on the Jew in the name of Christ. For this we can do no other than approach the Jew in deepest penitence. A separate chapter on the whole question of anti-Semitism is therefore called for.

Chapter Nine

ANTI-SEMITISM

Prof. A. Roy Eckardt begins his chapter on anti-Semitism with the heading "The Crime of Christendom." Perhaps this chapter should have been placed first in this volume. For the Christian has no right to say a word to the Jew without first openly recognizing and then seeking to atone for the appalling and perverted attitude of "Christendom," so-called, toward Jewry throughout the centuries. The very name Christendom signifies a way of life followed by a large section of the peoples of this globe, and bears within it reference to the name of Christ. The paradox is that outside of Christendom the Jews have frequently been much more welcome than within it. This evil thing within Christendom has persisted in the world ever since New Testament times; and despite Belsen and Buchenwald, it is present in the hearts of many even in this American area of what we still know as the Christian world.

No one is better qualified to deal with this fundamental issue than this professor at Lehigh University. He has written much on the subject already, and during the year 1963–1964 he made a fresh study of anti-Semitism in Britain and the countries of Europe. This chapter was actually written while he was resident in Cambridge, England.

—*The Editor*

There is no doubt that the Christian church's historical antipathy to "the Jews"[1] is one of the major roots of anti-Semitism in the Western world. Such authoritative historians as James Parkes and Jules Isaac have authenticated this fact indisputably; we need not establish it here but merely report it.[2]

I. The Crime of Christendom

The history of Christendom has involved culpable distortion of the true spiritual state of the synagogue and of the Jewish faith, not only respecting the period from Ezra to Jesus but down through the Christian centuries. It has meant unspeakable misrepresentation of "the wicked Jews" for allegedly rejecting "their" Messiah and indeed putting Jesus to death, the denial of the common humanity of Jews—something that is "the hallmark distinguishing anti-Semitism from other brands of prejudice"[3]—the "vulgar and unbridled abuse of Judaism and the Jewish people,"[4] and the horrible persecutions visited upon Jews at the direct or indirect instigation of Christian ecclesiastical authorities—in sum, an organized "system of degradation," and all in the name of divinely inspired truth.

[1] There is a trace of anti-Semitism, however unconscious, in the use of the article "the" before "Jews" at times when it would be quite sufficient to let the noun stand by itself.

[2] By James Parkes, among other works: *Antisemitism* (Quadrangle Books, Inc., 1963); *The Conflict of the Church and the Synagogue* (Meridian Books, 1961 [1934]); *The Foundations of Judaism and Christianity* (Quadrangle Books, Inc., 1960).

By Jules Isaac: *Genèse de l'Antisémitisme* (Paris: Calmann Lévy, 1956); *Has Anti-Semitism Roots in Christianity?* tr. by Dorothy and James Parkes (National Conference of Christians and Jews, 1961); *Jésus et Israël,* 2d ed. (Paris: Fasquelle, 1959); *The Teaching of Contempt* (Holt, Rinehart and Winston, Inc., 1964).

[3] Parkes, *The History of Jewish-Christian Relations* (an address to the London Society of Jews and Christians), unpublished, p. 10. We know that Negroes have often been regarded by whites as subhuman, yet this has not led to the conclusion that they should be exterminated. Their worst foes seem to find them at least useful as slaves, menials, or nurses for their children.

[4] Parkes, *The Foundations of Judaism and Christianity,* p. 226.

Jules Isaac sums up the entire spectacle in the phrase *the teaching of contempt,* "the most formidable and pernicious weapon ever used against Judaism or the Jews."[5] What makes Isaac's many citations so damning is that the overwhelming majority of them are from twentieth-century Christian writers and church authorities, and many of the statements have appeared *since* the defeat of the Nazis and the end of the Second World War. Theology—including the theology of the New Testament—is quite entitled to go beyond historical fact, but only when it "respects history as its point of departure"; this is "its sacred duty." The teaching of contempt involves three main doctrines: the Jewish Dispersion as punishment for the crucifixion, the degenerative state of the Jewish religion in the time of Jesus, and "the Jews" as a "deicide race." The first of these notions is patently false—"a theological myth without the slightest foundation."[6] The speciousness of the assertion of Judaism's degeneracy in Jesus' time has been convincingly demonstrated. With respect to the teaching of a "deicide race," no like allegation has ever been more persistent or issued in greater harm to human beings. (Is there, indeed, another allegation like unto this one?) Beyond its absurd assumption that Jesus must have revealed himself to the entire Jewish people "in the fullness of his divine nature" and been irresponsibly spurned by them, this allegation flouts the fact that Jesus died the victim of Roman authority. "Nothing, not even the cooperation of the Jewish authorities, can extenuate the significance of this historical fact, whose certainty is beyond question."[7]

[5] Isaac, *The Teaching of Contempt,* p. 34.

[6] A "myth" that lacks any genuine association with history should be identified not as myth but as legend. Isaac really means "legend" but he fails to make the distinction.

As Isaac points out, there were many dispersions of Jews from Palestine long before Christianity, there was no final dispersion either in A.D. 70 or A.D. 135, and in truth there has never been a final dispersion. See also James Parkes, *End of an Exile: Israel, the Jews and the Gentile World* (London: Vallentine, Mitchell & Co., Ltd., 1954), Ch. 4 on the continuity of Jewish life in Palestine since Roman times.

[7] Isaac, *The Teaching of Contempt,* pp. 39 ff., 144.

It would be well if evil legends could die a just death; as we shall see, the rational-historical hope that facts will set men free is challenged by psychic and sinful necessity. It would have been well, too, if the church, perhaps grown a little alarmed over the cancerous spread of its teaching of contempt and a bit conscience-stricken in the face of new humanitarian movements, could somehow have kept the whole matter within properly "religious" bounds. Someday the fruits of calumny might be turned against the church itself! But the hour proved too late. The world had been listening for a long time. And not only did the world learn the lessons ostensibly intended only for believers; it was to put these lessons to active use. Who says that "religious education" can exert no influence beyond the circle of the "faithful"! What was it that made possible the "greatest demonstration of the power of darkness the world has ever witnessed"?[8] We need not lay the entire blame for the Nazi murders of Jews at the door of the church in order to confess that the church has borne an incalculable share of that blame. For without the agelong bias of Christendom, anti-Semitism "would never have been able to inflame the passions of whole nations that have, at least nominally, been christianized for centuries. . . . Instead of confronting the world with God's Christ as the Jew dying for the world's sin, the Church presents the nations with a picture of the Jews betraying and killing the Christ Messiah," thus insuring the world's hatred of Jews.[9] When the initial Nazi measures against Jews were instituted in 1933, how was it possible for the propagandist Julius Streicher to identify what was occurring as Jewish punishment for Golgotha? Hermann Diem portrays the situation: When the sentiment, "His blood be on us and on our children"—through which Jews had allegedly prearranged a future divine judgment upon themselves!—was presented

[8] H. D. Leuner, *The Impact of Nazism on European Jewry* (Geneva: Committee on the Church and the Jewish People, World Council of Churches, 1962), p. 23.

[9] *Ibid.*, p. 24.

in the form of a watchword to the German people, Christian circles "were thrown into such confusion that any effective resistance to the anti-Jewish measures was rendered impossible. For it was with precisely the same watchword that the church over a period of nineteen hundred years had not only rationalized and justified but also advanced the hatred of Jews. . . . The seed which we ourselves had sown had sprung up, and we stood uncomprehending before its terrible fruits."[10]

James Parkes sums up the matter: "The fact that the action of Hitler and his henchmen was not really motivated by Christian sentiments, the fact that mingled with the ashes of murdered Jews are the ashes of German soldiers who refused to obey orders when they found out what those orders were, the fact that churches protested and that Christians risked their lives to save Jews—all these facts come into the picture, but unhappily they do not invalidate the basic statement that anti-Semitism from the first century to the twentieth is a Christian creation and a Christian responsibility, whatever secondary causes may come into the picture.[11] Whether they are serious Christians or not, men are inescapably afflicted by the propaganda and prejudices of a "Christian" culture.

Were any new evidence needed of the crime of Christendom, it would be more than fully attested by the latter-day reversal within the contemporary church. The reference here is not primarily to publicly circulated pronunciamentos, although these do carry a certain acknowledgment of sin and

[10] Hermann Diem, *Das Rätsel des Antisemitismus* (Munich: Chr. Kaiser Verlag, 1960), pp. 5–6, my translation. Diem seems almost to be suggesting that moral "confusion" is an all-sufficient excuse for lack of all moral resistance to evil. Such an implication is entirely improper. It appears inconceivable that in Germany, with its tradition of enlightenment and liberal Biblical criticism, there was no sentiment among Christians opposing a literalistic and indeed superstitious rendering of the "watchword" of Matt. 25:27. The fact remains that the last two sentences quoted from Diem make the citation fully appropriate at this juncture.

[11] Parkes, *The History of Jewish-Christian Relations,* p. 3.

guilt. Recently, I sat in a Jewish audience and heard a Christian speaker allude to the World Council of Churches' declaration at New Delhi that anti-Semitism is "sin against God and man." He also mentioned the date (although he failed to state that this was a reaffirmation demanded by continuing anti-Semitism). I shall not soon forget the way in which the audience received this word. They must have recognized much more than the fact that saying something is wrong does not change it. They must have sensed that when the obvious and the overdue are combined, the end result is the ludicrous. By *1961* the time had been put hopelessly out of joint. And so the audience *laughed*. And their laughter sounded like the laughter of judgment.

The reference is, rather, to the noteworthy drive within the church to set its own house in order. Thus, on the Protestant side the literature of religious education is being subjected to careful search with the aim of excising the very misrepresentations that an earlier time treated as truth integral and necessary to the propagation of the gospel.[12] On the Roman Catholic side we find a corresponding examination of educational literature and also the removal of offensive elements from the liturgy.[13] The church is at last starting to learn the contradiction in making verbal denunciations of anti-Semitism while providing practical insurance for the malady.[14] The beginnings of self-examination and repentance have come only after the deluge. But they have come.

[12] See Bernhard E. Olson, *Faith and Prejudice* (Yale University Press, 1963). This study shows, among other things, that adverse images of Jews in Protestant educational literature almost without exception reproduce stereotypes from earlier Christian history. See also Walter Neidhart, "The Fight Against Anti-Semitism in Christian Education," *The Ecumenical Review,* XV, 1 (October, 1962), pp. 57–66.

[13] St. Louis University has completed a self-study of Catholic textbooks. For reference to some recent liturgical changes, see Gregory Baum, *The Jews and the Gospel* (The Newman Press, 1961), pp. 9–10, 267.

[14] We need not deny all value to public statements by the church. Christian theology and common sense attest together that word and deed are subject to no final separation. Much depends upon what is said, the way in which it is said, the timing involved, and the extent of

II. The War of the Pagans Against the People of God

If theology must take history with great seriousness, we cannot conclude that it is history which dictates all theological insight. Weighty and lamentable reasons sustain the belief that even if the church had by some miracle of grace avoided its denigration of Jews, there would still be anti-Semitism in the world. The irrationality, fury, and terrible persistence of this evil embody an unparalleled form of social perversion. Nor can we ignore the issue of the presence of anti-Semitism beyond the Christian domain. The inner substance of hostility to Jews derives from much more than religious-historical pressures; it involves a spiritual trespass of great magnitude. This means that it is a theological question in two senses: (1) It is an aspect of the perennial struggle between man and God. (2) Theology seeks—amid its own sins and shortcomings—to grapple with and to fathom the mystery of human iniquity in the presence of God.

Are we merely the children of historical events (real or reputed) and of religious indoctrination? Is there not—somewhere within the obscure reaches of human freedom—a potentiality for deep conflict that transcends the temporal plane? It is incumbent upon us to be much more precise here than simply to attest that "man is a sinful being," i.e., that he commits evil deeds against his fellows. For this latter persuasion contains only generalized moral implications rather than concrete ones: one day Gentiles vilify "the Jews," another day white men exploit Negroes. The classic Biblical

---

effort to ensure that the words are put into living practice. A declaration given preliminary sanction at the Second Vatican Council on November 20, 1964, emphasizes that Christ died because of the sins of all men. From the standpoint of moral force, this emphasis is on quite a different level from that part of the same statement which merely repeats the truism that the church disapproves of anti-Semitism. Perhaps we may hope that the Christian church as a whole will one day move beyond a mere attribution of the death of Jesus to an abstract "humanity," and will confess openly its own sin for ever having treated the Jewish people as "blind" and "heinous."

doctrine of sin was always meant to be theological and concrete. It was an existential report of the war against God, that judge and guardian of men's true but unrecognized destiny. Further, any generalizing emphasis upon "man's inhumanity to man" is succeeded by an awesome concentration: The rebellion against *this* God is turned upon the *people* who are his representatives (*Stellvertreter*) before the world. And these people are not just anyone. They are "the *Jews*."

How do Jews represent God and why does this lead to enmity? The Jewish reality means rejection of paganism and a summons of obedience to the Lord of heaven and earth. One way to gain comprehension of this truth is by reference to the two categories of *time* and *space*, "the main structures of existence to which all existing things are subjected."[15]

In large measure, human history and the human soul are fashioned by the struggle between time and space. Paganism means the elevation of a particular space to ultimate glory. Its god is bound to a particular place and therefore stands in conflict, not just with other spatial deities, but more tellingly with a truly unconditional deity. The command to Abraham to leave the homeland of his fathers meant a summons to surrender the gods of soil and blood, of family, tribe, and nation, for the sake of the universal God who transcends spatial restrictions. Through Abraham all the families of the earth are one day to be blessed. The prophetic threat, first heard in the message of Amos, represents the turning point in the history of religion; it is unheard of that the God of a nation will destroy that nation without being himself destroyed. The ultimate point in the struggle between time and space is the monotheism of justice. The gods of space necessarily oppose justice, for their unlimited claims destroy the universalism implied by the idea of justice. The meaning of prophetic monotheism, by contrast, is that God is one because justice is one.[16]

[15] Paul Tillich, *Theology of Culture*, edited by R. C. Kimball (Oxford University Press, 1959), p. 30.

[16] A summary and interpretive paraphrase of *ibid.*, pp. 30–38, *passim.*

Anti-Semitism is a method of human retribution against God for daring to get in the way of man's imagined autonomy, with his drive to master his own destiny. To be confronted by Jewry is to be met by the holy God of justice, in some measure through conscious realization but more importantly through the collective unconscious. As Will Herberg affirms: "Anti-Semitism is the other side of the election and vocation of Israel, the revolt of the pagan against the God of Israel and his absolute demand, one of the ways—the typical symbolic way—in which the pagan 'gods of space' revenge themselves on the people of the 'Lord of time.' "[17]

"The Jew is, whether he will or not, a standing reproach to the pagan in man and society, an unassimilable element in any culture engaged in deifying itself—and he is that simply by *being a Jew* and quite apart from his personal faith or desire. . . . The choice for him is authentic or unauthentic Jewish existence, God's witness in self-affirmation or in self-repudiation—but God's witness he remains nevertheless. Such is the 'mystery of Israel.' "[18]

The Jewish people are the servants who suffer for the King of the universe, scapegoats standing in the place of the Holy One—although woe betide their detractors! How intense is the irony: The gods of space must finally obey man (they are, after all, his own fabrications) as through the tendency of finite reality to "sink into itself"[19] humanity is enslaved, whereas the true God calls men to the only obedience that will set them free. Jewry may, of course, fall into its own idolatries,[20] but the essential fact remains that by its

[17] Will Herberg, *Judaism and Modern Man* (Farrar, Straus & Young, Inc., 1951), pp. 273, 274.

[18] Herberg, "Judaism and Christianity: Their Unity and Difference," *The Journal of Bible and Religion,* XXI, 2 (April, 1953), p. 72.

[19] Leonhard Ragaz, *Israel, Judaism and Christianity* (London: Victor Gollancz, Ltd., 1947), p. 10.

[20] For possible "spatial" elements within Judaism, see Tillich, *op. cit.,* pp. 38–39, and cf. A. Roy Eckardt, *Christianity and the Children of Israel* (King's Crown Press, 1948), pp. 38–39. The sense in which Zionism and the establishment of the State of Israel may or may not manifest the invasion of the values of "space" into Jewish reality is beyond the limits of our subject; cf. Eckardt, *op. cit.,* pp. 163–172.

very existence, it testifies to the holy, sovereign God. Here is its peace, yet here is its enmity.

III. The War of Christians Against Jesus the Jew

Ambivalence seldom maintains an even balance of love and hate; witness the parent who dies for the rejected child, but witness too the lover scorned who destroys his beloved. And witness now the enmity of the younger brother for the elder.

That God's own people should be held to repudiate the "true faith" tips the scales in behalf of hatred. That the origin and center of this faith should be himself a *Jew* works to displace any weight that remains for the love which is patient and kind, which does not insist on its own way, and is never resentful.

What is all this business of "confronting the world with God's Christ as the Jew dying for the world's sin"? Does the world have the slightest interest in being confronted in that fashion? The world would rather think quite differently of itself: To be sure, there might be something a *little* wrong with me (no one is perfect), but what is this nonsense about my being a *sinner?* And more to the point, what could be more reprehensible than the prospect of a *Jew* dying for *me?* It is downright contaminating.

God summons men to obedience that they may be blessed. The Christian dispensation reaffirms this statement, but it relies upon certain "things which have been accomplished among us" as a means of expanding the subject of the statement: God was in Christ reconciling unto himself those erstwhile strangers to the covenant of promise, the Christ who tells those who would come after him that they must deny themselves and take up their cross.[21] Thus, this Christ brings not alone the divine forgiveness but also the divine imperative of self-abnegation. We may welcome the forgiveness all right—although that in itself forces the admission of our

[21] Luke 1:1; II Cor. 5:19; Eph. 2:12; Matt. 16:24.

wrongness—and still reject the demand. In denying the demand, we deny Christ, yet we cannot very well put our hands on him directly. However, we can get at him through *other* Jews, the ones for whom he is the inevitable reminder and inescapable archetype. (They *remind* as well the rowdy who bombs or defaces a synagogue, and who has not the remotest concern for Christianity or allegiance to the church.) Hatred must be enacted; it has no peace to hold and it cannot hold its tongue: "So you claim to be God's people? Well, you *may* have been, once upon a time. But you are his people no longer! Christ-killers!" A more qualified scapegoat is simply unimaginable. We project upon "the Jews" our own hatred of Christ. Yet to utilize "the Jewish crucifixion" of Christ both as a means of ridding ourselves of Christ and of exonerating any trespass of ours is to aggravate our plight, for in continuing to punish Jews we merely sharpen the apprehension of our guilt over having rejected Christ in them. This greater guilt can only mean greater opposition to those who externally represent our own internal rejection of Christ. It is even possible that a genuine desire to accept Christ may compound our anti-Semitism, since the reception of his forgiveness seems (heretically, of course) contingent upon our own purification, made possible through the displacing of our sin upon the scapegoat. Thus our wish to accept Christ joins forces with our need to reject him, and the circle's viciousness is completed.

Is all the above no more than speculation? Is theology here being run through the intricacies and confusions of a psychoanalytic maze? While it is certainly true that the interpretation sketched above is subject to no final proof, it does rest upon a rather formidable experiential and historical base: The rights of the elder brother *were* established before the younger brother was ever born; Christianity *does* rest upon a thoroughly Jewish foundation. Jesus *was* a Jew. He *does* make absolute demands upon the Christian conscience. And from the standpoint of both duration and intensity no people has *ever* been subjected to the persecutions which "the Jews" have met within Christendom. One cannot, of course, secure the validity of a particular interpretation upon the shortcomings of other views. Yet he can offer that interpretation as a point of departure for raising pertinent and pointed questions: Is it not hauntingly possible that one reason the Christian world failed to oppose Nazi anti-Semitism was its own ambivalent attitude toward "the Jews" and toward the Jew Jesus? How are we to account for the fact that Christians have been not only rather morbidly fascinated by "the Jewish question," but fall such easy victims to anti-Semitic feelings and behavior?[22] Why is it that the people from whom the church's Christ came are the very ones that Christendom has oppressed so horribly?[23]

IV. The End and the Beginning

The complicity of the Christian centuries does not seem able to account alone for the power of anti-Semitism. However, it will be observed that such questions as those listed just above both bespeak a connection with interpretations offered by the psychology of depth and recall us to the very concentration upon history that is required by the limitations inherent in a purely generalizing emphasis upon "prejudice."

Ernst Simmel asserts from the standpoint of psychopathological theory: "The Jew must take over the role of innocent lamb, carrying the load of hate which up to now has not been absorbed in the process of Christian civilization. The anti-Semite who tortures and kills the Jew actually re-enacts the crucifixion of his Savior."[24] Freud expresses the matter in

[22] A. Roy Eckardt, "The Theology of Anti-Semitism," *Religion in Life,* XXI, 4 (Autumn, 1962), 555.

[23] *Ibid.,* p. 557. The relation between the Jewish and Christian faiths has important bearing upon the problem of anti-Semitism, but that relation cannot be pursued here. On this whole matter, see Will Herberg, *Judaism and Modern Man,* and A. Roy Eckardt, *The Elder and the Younger Brother: Dimensions of the Jewish-Christian Encounter* (Holt, Rinehart and Winston, Inc., 1965).

[24] Ernst Simmel, in *Anti-Semitism: A Social Disease* (International Universities Press, Inc., 1946), p. 61.

terms of the two religions: "The hatred of Judaism is at bottom hatred for Christianity."[25] Anti-Semitism must finally turn against Christianity, for there is no Christianity apart from Jesus the Jew.

An association of historical analysis and theological analysis is suggested in Bernhard E. Olson's multiple contention that Jules Isaac tends to underestimate pre-Christian anti-Semitism, that in the ancient world Jews "were the sole and zealous protagonists of religious monotheism," and that pagan anti-Semitism insinuated itself into the church with the influx of Gentiles.[26] H. Sachar writes: "The European Christian cannot forgive the Jew for giving him Christianity. . . . It is not because . . . they are 'good Christians' that the Europeans are instinctively antisemites. It is because they are bad Christians, in reality repressed . . . pagans."[27] (In this as in other respects, Americans must also be considered "Europeans.") And Franz Rosenzweig's words come inevitably to mind: "Whenever the pagan within the Christian soul rises in revolt against the yoke of the Cross, he vents his fury on the Jew."[28]

"Solutions" are beyond the compass of interpretation here, yet several related considerations are in order: (1) The morphology of anti-Semitism as herein described is destroyed implicitly through what has been said about it. The defeat of a unique force lies, in principle, within that force's unique opposite. We begin with *honesty,* concerning history and ourselves, and we end in the *adoration* of the Lord and *openness* to his strange power. To fling Christ's summons away is chimera itself and the devil's own trap, for Christ's grace is the unconditioned foe of anti-Semitism. To receive that

[25] Sigmund Freud, *Moses and Monotheism,* tr. by K. Jones (Alfred A. Knopf, Inc., 1939), p. 145.

[26] Bernhard E. Olson, Introductory Essay to Isaac's *Has Anti-Semitism Roots in Christianity?* pp. 14, 15.

[27] H. Sachar, "Revenge on the Prophets: A Psychoanalysis of Anti-Semitism," *Menorah Journal,* XXVIII, 3 (Fall, 1940), as quoted in Herberg, *Judaism and Modern Man,* p. 284.

[28] Franz Rosenzweig, as quoted in Herberg, "Judaism and Christianity: Their Unity and Difference," p. 74.

grace, we need wait for no *eschaton;* to wait is to presuppose that we are now damned. (2) Suppose that one day we must face the agony of choice between the "true faith" and reconciliation with our elder brother. I speak for no one save myself here, but I believe that I shall pray for the courage to choose reconciliation, in the name of Jesus Christ himself. For we cannot work around our disavowal of Christ; we can only pierce through it to something else. And the only provision we may ourselves bring for the journey is a handclasp with the brother we have wronged. (3) The "personal" dimension of our faith reaches out, that it may be completed. In Christian faith we are always skirting the edge of a morally inconsequential pietism. And we break the tension between Christian and Jewish elements in Christianity whenever we forget that justice is the only social instrument of love. But when we remember this instrument, we establish a common front with all men who work to alleviate anti-Semitism. (4) The main contributions of Christian thought within the struggle are, on the one hand, to ensure against the idealism and the pessimism that are the twin temptations of secular interpretation, and, on the other hand, to attest to the uniqueness of anti-Semitism in the light of historical and theological understanding. (5) Can the church be made ready to lose its life—*all* its life: its programs, its successes, its powers and privileges? Perhaps not. Probably not. But, then, where are the *Stellvertreter* of him who made himself of no reputation and gave himself for the lost? Could it be that the end of Christendom's time is his victory?

Chapter Ten

BEYOND DIALOGUE

This chapter was written by the Editor of the volume only after all the other chapters were complete, and only after full consultation with most of the other authors.

We are living in a time when Roman Catholics and Protestants have entered into a new experience of mutual respect and understanding. The authors of this volume believe that the Spirit of the living God is also seeking to lead us as Jews and Christians along an equally significant path. Yet this path, by the nature of things, will not be easy to walk. Present-day attempts at reconciliation between Jew and Christian are vitiated by the memory of past hatreds and by often unfortunate proselytizing programs. What Jews and Christians ought to seek to do together, however, on the level of their respective "Highest Common Factors," despite the past, and for the sake of a world that does not yet believe, is the subject of this final discussion.

—*The Editor*

Some of the preceding chapters have been of a theological nature, others have been factual and informative. Both approaches to the question of right relationships between Jews and Christians are necessary. North Americans are naturally more interested in pragmatic solutions to problems than in theoretical discussion. But with respect to the issue before us, the practical depends upon the theological; for the "mystery" of Israel rests in this, that the Jewish people cannot be finally explained in either political, sociological, or even religious terms, but only in theological. For Israel is the People of *God*.

In the light of this unique fact, let us now turn to the situation that obtains in countless suburban areas in North America, where Jews and Christians live together as neighbors and as friends. What is to be the Christian's attitude toward his Jewish neighbor, and what is he as a Christian meant to say and do in the presence of his friend?

I. What Is Asked of the Christian

In the first place, the Christian ought to be an informed churchman. It is only politeness, to say the least, to read, even in a cursory manner, the story of the wandering Jew between the fall of Jerusalem in A.D. 70 and the arrival, beginning in the last century, of Jewish immigrants in America. Much prejudice and misunderstanding can be got rid of by the unearthing of the facts of the Jewish story. But even as he reads up, or hears a lecture upon, the story of the development of the ghetto in Europe, and learns of the appalling manner in which Christendom, so-called, has treated the "heretical," "unbelieving," "nonconformist" Jew, the Christian comes to acknowledge, with a deep sense of shame, the unspeakable sins of his forefathers. He learns that he has inherited from their medieval, uninformed prejudices, deep in his own subconscious mind, anti-Jewish sentiments that can have no place in the mind of a follower of Christ. A few lectures or discussion groups on the *facts* of the Jewish past, done jointly between local church and local synagogue, can act as a true catharsis in the mind of the Gentile community, and bring the Christian who is willing to accept rebuke to a wholesome sense of shame and contrition.

One effect of such a study of Jewish-Christian relations in the past has been to open the eyes of the Christian to a sympathetic understanding of why it is that the Jew may completely misunderstand the Christian faith. Jews like to repeat the words of Jesus: "By their fruits ye shall know them." The story of the Christian church in its relationships with the synagogue has been the chief obstacle that prevents Jews from discovering what we see in Jesus.

II. Jewish Objections to Christianity

Secondly, through study of his Jewish neighbors and of their faith the Christian should learn to understand the objections to Christian beliefs that many Jews entertain. This is salutary for both parties. The Jew very rightly and quite naturally is furnished with answers, if he asks for them, to the stock arguments of the Christian. For example, there are available for him in print Jewish replies to the traditional arguments used by literalistic Christians that seek to "prove" Christ from Old Testament prophecy. Christians should always remember that when Jesus asked his disciples the question: "Who do men say that I am?" the argument from prophecy gave them no help at all.

On the other hand, if the Christian seeks even for his own satisfaction to give an answer to the objections the Jew can raise to Christian beliefs, then the reality of his own faith is tested, and he can be mightily strengthened and confirmed therein. Yet what right, we may ask, has the exponent of any faith to offer it to another man, provided the latter already possesses a faith, and is not an agnostic, unless he has first studied to know wherein the other finds his roots? Judaism is the *only* major non-Christian religion in North America. Therefore, the Christian ought to do Judaism the honor of discovering what it really *is*.

Let me suggest a few of these objections. As we read these and learn of still others not listed here, we are to keep rigorously in mind that every man theologizes within a framework of reference which he has inherited, possibly adapted, and then made his own. In the Middle Ages, Christians could not grasp the idea that Jews could *sincerely* think differently from themselves, and supposed that the Jews could only be perverse in not grasping Christian truths as Christians understood them. And, be it said, Jews thought Christians to be equally perverse for not seeing the truth as only Jews could see it. As twentieth-century citizens, however, we would now be wrong to fall back into such a subjective view of another man's frame of reference. Jewish objections to Christian theology, then, are made *sincerely,* and not from perversity.

1. "Christianity, with its worship of two (or three) Gods, is an 'aberration of the pure monotheism' of Judaism." Perhaps we could find a bridge of understanding with the Jew who makes such a declaration (Chapter 7 of this volume).

2. "Jesus is a false Messiah. He has not accomplished what the Messiah is expected to accomplish, viz., set up the Kingdom of God upon earth." The Christian ought never to seek to "refute" Jewish objections. Chapter 4 offers a common basis of discussion for both Jew and Christian on what the word "Messiah" really means.

3. "Jesus is not the Savior, for the world is still unsaved." Chapter 7, II, leads both Jew and Christian to the feet of the one God, the Father of both, and the Savior of the world.

4. "Christianity is wrong in respect to its doctrine of original sin. Every man is born innocent, is capable of communing with God, and enters the world without taint." Some Christians misconceive their own faith here, being unaware of the Old Testament view of sin. Our Chapter 2 examines this question in the light of our fellowship with our Jewish neighbor.

5. "There is no need for any mediator between God and man, for God has given man the privilege of direct access to himself." Chapter 5 deals with this issue.

6. "The doctrine of vicarious atonement is immoral. God deals with each man according to justice and merit." See Chapter 5 again.

7. "Paul misunderstood Judaism when he declared that the law is a curse or a snare; or if he himself is misunder-

stood in this matter, at least he declared that the law was obsolete and defunct." (Where did Paul say this?)

8. "Christians say that the Old Covenant has been annulled. This cannot be so, for the survival of the Jewish people proves the opposite." We deal with this problem fully in Chapter 2.

9. "The New Testament adds nothing new to the teaching contained in the Old Testament. For example, the Golden Rule had already been laid down before Jesus' days by Jewish rabbis." This should be a source of joy to us that it should be so. Yet we recall that Christianity is not primarily a moral system, but is the gospel for sinners. See Chapter 6.

10. "Christian ethics is impracticable. The Sermon on the Mount is exaggerated idealism." The Christian realizes, however, that this question must be seen in the light of the resurrection of Christ and the life of the Kingdom which he offers.

11. "Jesus said: 'My kingdom is not of this world.' Judaism looks to *this* world for the realization of the Kingdom." The Christian believes, however, on the basis of the Old Testament which he shares with the Jew, that the "other world" has no meaning apart from "this world."

Perhaps the previous chapters have not thrown sufficient light on all these issues, and there are many more; but a thoughtful and prayerful reading of them and then group discussion upon them, using the Bible as a guide, should open up new vistas of understanding of both the Christian and the Jewish faith.

III. The Christian Dilemma

In any local situation, Christians and Jews should approach each other, not from positions of strength, but from humility and concern. Thus the Christian should never feel that the Jew ought to become a Christian on the ground that Christianity is the dominant faith, or because "Christianity is the religion of the Americas." Indeed, if the Christian rightly understands his faith, the very idea of "strength" is wholly misleading. For the Christian serves One who came to be the Servant, and not the Master, of the world.

Yet the sincere and honest Christian becomes acquainted with a deep tension in his mind when he seeks to make confrontation with his Jewish neighbor in sincere dialogue, the Jew as a Jew, and he as a Christian, and both not just as fellow citizens or members together of the local P.T.A. For the Christian is unshakably convinced that Jesus is the Light of the *world,* and that God, *in Christ,* has acted for the salvation of *all men.* How, then, is he to talk to his Jewish friend, remaining true to this basic conviction, and yet remain completely courteous and gentlemanly in his respect for the faith of his friend?

Chapter 5 outlined for us "the advantage of the Jew," a phrase that Paul uses in Rom. 3:1. If we have ever sought to share in words with the typical modern agnostic our delight in being alive, or tried to meet him at that point in life where man ought to feel the mystery of existence and the joy of knowing that that mystery is benign, we have met with sad frustration. For how can a man speak French with another who knows no French? But the advantage of the Jew is just that he possesses so much that the agnostic knows nothing about. Paul goes on to declare that to the Jew belong "the adoption, and the glory, and the covenants, and the giving of the law, and the service of God, and the promises; whose are the fathers" (Rom. 9:4–5). This means that as Christians we share with the Jews the whole area of grace and the whole area of freedom. I remember crossing Europe in a slow train just before war broke out, sitting for hours on a third-class wooden bench, and finding myself in the constant company of men *with whom I had nothing in common,* for they were Nazis. And then I met a man squeezed into a corner, who informed me apologetically that he was a Jew. My heart leaped out to him, and I found his also to mine, once he discovered that I was a Christian, and not a Nazi, for we possessed *in common* that great list of advantages which we have just quoted. What we are to realize is that the Christian is closer even to the *un*believing Jew (this is a strange paradox) than he is to the unbelieving Gentile; therefore, how much closer to the believing Jew he is, it is his joyous privilege to discover.

IV. How Can We Resolve the Dilemma?

This strange and wonderful but God-given fact pulls the Christian up short if he supposes that his duty is to "proselytize" his Jewish neighbor. The word has acquired ugly associations for the North American Jew, who may recall past experiences in Europe at the hands of sectarian groups or from an Eastern European Church, even if he has only learned of these from a grandparent. We recall that Christ himself objected to it as it was exemplified by some Pharisees of his day (Matt. 23:15). As a sincere Jewish educator said to the principal of a church school to which he sent his child: "I commit her to your care, for I know that a true Christian cannot and will not proselytize any more than he can be an anti-Semite." For proselytism, in the sense in which Jews have experienced it, implies a basic scorn for the faith of the other man; and he who practices it exhibits that he is affected with a form of fanaticism, in that he believes that he alone possesses the whole truth. We have only to remind ourselves of the objectionable activities of certain sects to recognize how un-Christlike proselytism can be. The average thoughtful Christian can look back over the years and trace a growth and development in his own faith from meager beginnings up to a wider and deeper understanding of the ways of God. But he remembers how the youth he once was, at the age of twenty, was then absolutely convinced that he was right in what he believed, and the memory of this dogmatism that he then entertained now makes him humble.

The Christian, then, has come to see that it is not his own limited understanding of the Christian faith which he should offer to the Jew, for that is a changing quantity; it must be Jesus Christ alone. He is then faced with the following problem: ought he to proclaim the fact of Christ, or "herald" it, to use a Pauline verb, and in this way be true to his calling as a Christian, which is to *evangelize?* As it is, the Jew, in mixed company, consistently declares that Judaism alone truly witnesses to the unity of God. The Christian remembers his Lord's command: "Go ye into all the world, and preach the gospel to every creature" (Mark 16:15); then he wonders what the words "preach the gospel" and "evangelize" really mean, especially in connection with his Jewish neighbor. He recognizes that they cannot mean "argue against," or "browbeat intellectually," or "present a set of propositions" about Christ, such as that "there is none other name under heaven given among men whereby we must be saved" (Acts 4:12)—even if such a proposition is true for him. Anyway, he is secretly aware both of the futility of any such "evangelism," and of an innate distaste for such a venture.

Again we may envisage ourselves as individuals or think of our congregation as a unit, seeking to "evangelize" the members of the local synagogue, and in doing so recognize a condescending tone and an ingratiating manner creeping into our approach. From this viewpoint was not Prof. Reinhold Niebuhr justified in making the statement which we read in Chapter 8, page 150?

But then, is this really what the Bible itself means by "evangelism"? Many Jews themselves do not think so. As a leading American rabbi declared on learning of Dr. Niebuhr's dictum: "If I were a Christian, I could not say what Niebuhr said." For the Jew who stays close to the Bible, as does this rabbi, knows that the Christian faith is not a philosophy about God; rather, it is a commitment to God who has acted in history and revealed himself in Christ. Thus it means complete obedience to his summons to proclaim his love and compassion for humanity to all men everywhere. When, therefore, the church ceases to be missionary-minded, it ceases in reality to be the church; it becomes instead a mere club for like-minded people of a religious turn of mind.

V. The Church's Missionary Commission

A century ago, the great Jewish theologian Salomon Formstecher declared that "Christianity was called to that powerful expression of the 'world soul,' which was *allowed* to represent the truth in hybrid form, to missionize the world for Judaism" (Hans Joachim Schoeps, *The Jewish-Christian Argument: A History of Theologies in Conflict,* tr. by David E. Green, p. 114, our italics). That is to say, he accepted the fact that Christianity was doing the missionary task that Israel of old had been called upon to do (cf. Isa. 49:6), and which modern Judaism appears to have no intention of doing; even though, not being a Christian, Formstecher had to posit that God only *allowed* Christianity to "represent the truth in hybrid form." One of the greatest modern exponents of Judaism, however, Franz Rosenzweig, just fifty years ago, felt compelled to admit what no Jew before him had ever admitted of his own free will (and, as Schoeps declares, *op. cit.,* pp. 141–142, without this Jewish admission no further discussion is possible between Jews and Christians) that not one of the nations of the world comes to the Father except through Jesus Christ. The Christian need never apologize, therefore, to the Jew for being missionary-minded. The Jew should expect it of him. Schoeps himself largeheartedly admits (*op. cit.,* p. 160) that the Christian mission to the world, one that must necessarily include the Jew, "cannot be traditionally grounded in such a way that it could become valid *halakhah,* but it can become *minhag,* which, in the realm of Judaism often enjoys respect equal, if not superior, to *halakhah.*" What he means is that an acceptance of the missionary nature of Christianity naturally could not be regarded as an article of belief by the Jew, but yet could be regarded as a thing true in itself. But the Christian expects the Jew, in return, to pay attention to this question—If it is in fact the fullness of the revelation of the love of God in Christ that has won the nations to the Father, then might not something be lacking in Judaism? For Israel was elected to be this very thing, viz., God's instrument through whom his salvation might reach to the ends of the earth. Moreover, the Christian would invite the Jew to ask himself the question, How can he claim to be already with the Father if being *with* God means doing what God himself does, viz., pour himself out in compassionate concern that *all* men might know his love?

The "advantage" that we share with the Jew, however, should be his consciousness and ours that the only right way to understand and practice the word "evangelism" is to follow the way of Ezekiel, that prophet of Israel whom we possess in common. For Ezekiel made the discovery that to evangelize his fellows with any effect at all, as he put it himself, "I sat where they sat" (Ezek. 3:15). This action is, of course, exactly what the Christian believes the Lord God Almighty chose to do in his incarnation in Christ. For God did not proclaim his love for man from the sky, meanwhile keeping at a safe distance from his rather distasteful humanity. He first involved himself in their daily life and thought, their hopes and tensions, fears and failures, and *in so doing,* he proclaimed, or heralded, his love, and thus "evangelized" his world.

In the same manner, then, we too are meant to *communicate* with our Jewish neighbor as well as with agnostics, Buddhists, and any other, not merely by means of proclaiming the gospel of Christ objectively, or to put it popularly, by offering him the gospel on a silver salver. Nor are we meant to proclaim merely *our* faith to the Jew or to anyone else. It is not what *we* believe that matters, although we are fully justified in talking about our faith with any Jewish or Gentile neighbor. And this for two reasons. First, faith must not be separated from love. The latter term, after all, is just another way of saying, "I sat where they sat." Unless love comes first, then "faith" cannot be transmitted. For loving a man is like learning his language. It means accepting him as a person. Second, it is not *what* we believe that we are to communicate, but *whom* we believe. In other words, there is one thing, and only one thing, that we must communicate to Jews as to all men, and that is Christ. To refrain from doing so, to imagine that while the quarreling Gentile family next door obviously needs Christ, the moral Jewish family does not, is a form of religious anti-Semitism which is as basically evil as the philosophy of the Nazis.

VI. Is Dialogue Enough?

The Christian, then, must be obedient to the revealed will of God, and so be ready to "preach Christ," "in season and out of season," as the New Testament puts it. Yet he must do so only in love and without discrimination against any group in the community—Negro, Jew, or any other. Does this mean, then, that he should do so by means of "dialogue," the term so beloved of modern man? Dialogue implies that two persons not only speak to each other, they also *listen* to each other. The latter element is essential, if, in love, we mean to respect each other's personality and beliefs. Indeed, then, the Christian should enter into dialogue with his Jewish friend, and he with him.

Now, dialogue as we need to understand it obviously does not mean discussion, open and frank, on the part of both parties, necessarily leading to an agreement on issues that concern them both. This conception of dialogue would be true in the case, say, of discussions between church and state, in the matter perhaps of religious observance in schools. The point is that in our case we are concerned with two persons standing *before God,* and who thus confront each other as sons of God. In such a case the one speaks to the other, not about himself, but about himself as he is related *to God,* and the other replies likewise; and so dialogue on the level that this volume has in view involves a triangular relationship, with God as the third party in the confrontation.

We have seen from earlier chapters why the Christian must listen to the Jew; for the Jew has so much to give to the Christian, even as the Christian has so much to give to the Jew. That is to say, "mission" cannot be a one-sided affair. The Jew wants to tell us about the Torah of God, which is so vitally important to him as revelation. And we must ask ourselves as we listen to him: Do I just tolerate this idea of his or do I really respect it? Is his view of revelation as valid as that which I believe God has given to me in Christ? The Rev. James Parkes, the noted English scholar of Jewish affairs, has made this position with clarity and judgment in a number of his books. There were two great moments in the world's history, he has written, when God revealed himself in saving action. The first was at Mt. Sinai, when, through his servant Moses, God elected Israel to be his People and laid in their hands his revealed will for man in the form of the law. The second was in the birth, life, teaching, death, and resurrection of Jesus Christ, who is both the incarnation of the living God and the Savior of the world. The second action of God in no way cancels out his first one. The two events are two poles of tension in the realm of revelation. They both represent the will of God and must continue to stand over each other in their opposition and yet agreement. The Christian therefore, Parkes asserts, has no right to any thought of superiority over the Jew, nor has he the right to approach him with the gospel, as if the gospel—for the Jew—were the completion of the law given at Sinai.

Yet, is this tolerant and kindly view of revelation in accord with the witness of the New Testament? As we saw in Chapter 2, the fullness that is in Christ *includes* the Torah, but does not abolish it; for Christ is the *plērōma,* the all-in-all, who fulfills all things in himself. If this is so, and it is the heart of the New Testament revelation, then the Christian cannot rest content even with dialogue, even when it is carried on in complete humility and love. We dare to say as much simply because the Christian does not offer on his side of the dialogue his own ideas about Christ and the Bible, far less his own experience of God's love and forgiveness; nor does he offer a "New Testament gospel for the individual" as against "the Old Testament corporate approach to

God." Both Testaments have an equally corporate understanding of the true relationship between God and his people. Ultimately, therefore, the Christian must go beyond the area of dialogue, for he must ceaselessly witness to the Christ who is greater than his own faith and greater than his own understanding of what Christianity may be. And, as we have seen, the Jew does not object to such witness, for he knows that it is essential to Christianity itself.

VII. The End of the "Cold War"

It is a matter of deep thankfulness that the Roman Catholic–Protestant "cold war" that has lasted for four hundred years has now ended, and that we have entered into a new era of sympathetic understanding of each other. Here our confidence in a new hope for the future rests in a most important new conception of the word "unity." For the convinced Protestant cannot conceive of himself becoming a Catholic or of "submitting" to Rome, nor can the convinced Catholic ever contemplate becoming a Protestant. But both Catholic and Protestant are now talking of *moving forward* toward a greater fullness, a new understanding of the *plērōma* could we say, one which will include the witness of all sections of Christendom that today exist in separation. But the churches will never be faithful to their ecumenical task until they direct their own hopes, and invite the Jewish people to do so also, toward a fullness that will include Jewry as well. Many theologians now feel that it was wrong to invite the Roman Catholic Church to observe at the New Delhi General Assembly of the World Council of Churches without inviting the Jews also. In his *Le Problème oecuménique* (2 vols., Paris), Fr. Bernard Lambert insists that the division between the church and Israel goes to the root of the separation in the church, for it affects not only the division between East and West, but also that between the Roman Catholic and the Evangelical Churches. Thus this Roman Catholic theologian does not make Rome the starting point for unity discussions, but Jerusalem. Chapter 8 has already quoted other Roman Catholic theologians who make this same point.

The city of Berlin is today divided by a wall that is very difficult to penetrate. Yet some Easterners do penetrate it in ones and twos almost daily. Those in the West then welcome them in and seek to make them feel at home in what they believe to be a truer democracy than that which they left behind. Perhaps their new friends turn a blind eye to the unwelcome news that some Westerners find the democracy of the East more to their liking, and cross over thither in the opposite direction. Yet no one believes that this traffic represents an ideal state of affairs, even though the "converts" in each case may be completely sincere, and are equally warmly welcomed by the community they join, and which believes that it alone is "right." The ideal, of course, would be the dismantling of the wall, and so rendering the German nation one, as it is meant to be.

Now, the New Testament makes the affirmation that "the wall" is in fact down (Eph. 2:14), and that all men—Jews, Christians, and agnostics alike—are already one in the fullness of Christ. The trouble is, of course, that none of us really believes it. Despite our unbelief, however, it is obviously our duty to live and to behave in the atmosphere of this new situation, now that the wall *is down.*

In the face of this fact, that the wall *is down,* Jewish-Christian relationships take on a new light. This light reveals to our eyes that it is not our task to preside at the funeral of Judaism, nor to take from the Jew his joy in the Torah, any more than it is his to take from us the cross of Christ. For in the *plērōma*—the fullness that the New Testament speaks of—it is shown to be legitimate to exhibit differentiation; that is to say, not differentiation in terms of mutuality, but certainly in terms of vocation. Just as a man has a vocation before God different from a woman's, so the Hebraic heritage of the Jew in his reverence for the Torah is a vocation that he must not disclaim. Consequently, even when the Jew does not see things as we see them, it is incumbent upon us as Christians, by our conversation, in our theology, and through our life hidden with Christ in God, to witness to him that *the wall is down,* and so, perhaps even mutely, to invite him to bring his special calling into the fullness *which already includes all that both he and we have to offer.* That fullness is therefore not represented by the Baptist, Methodist, Episcopal, Roman Catholic, or any other Church. A united Germany will be greater than the sum of its two parts. That fullness is Christ alone, and to him the whole Israel of God is called to witness (Isa. 2:1–4; Acts 1:8).

VIII. The "Sister Faiths"

Enough has been said in this volume to make clear the Christian's claim that Christianity is not the "daughter of Judaism." A daughter would be ungenerous if she thought she could witness to what her mother did not know. Judaism and Christianity are, rather, sisters, for they are both daughters of the faith that they share in common from the pages of the Old Testament. One of the important signs of the times, therefore, and one that gives us a deep sense of joy as we look into the future, is the fact of the rediscovery, not just of the Torah, but of the Old Testament as a whole, by both Jews and Christians. The postwar rise in eager study of Biblical theology has been the most significant bridge that has ever been thrown across the gap that lies between us. And it is a feature of North American Jewry, as something distinct from Israeli and European Jewry, that this is so. Thus it is obvious that Jews and Christians ought to be studying the Old Testament *together,* something which is already happening in the learned societies. Such study elicits evangelism, proclamation, confrontation, dialogue, and witness by both parties all in one. But it does not turn evangelism into imperialism. We should remember that the Jew has as strongly held interpretations of the Old Testament to offer the Christian as the Christian has to offer him. But since God himself is love, God's love is present in the hearts of both parties when they study his Word together—for they are studying within that "city" across which there runs no middle wall of partition (Gal. 3:28–29).

The *Orthodox Jew* knows the Bible through the Talmud, and believes that the tradition enshrined in it is the will of God for the Jew as a Jew. Yet, ultimately, he does not worship that tradition. It is just *Mishnah,* which means "the repetition of the Torah," as the revealed will of God. He worships God himself.

The *Conservative Jew,* loyally seeking to adapt his ancient heritage to the very different life of twentieth-century America, is making a great effort to align the Talmudic tradition with the modern world. Yet in all that he does he is seeking to be obedient, not to the Torah, but to God himself; and to that extent he is returning afresh to the source of his knowledge in the Old Testament.

The *Reform Jew* has discarded tradition to a degree his Conservative brethren cannot follow. But in so doing, he is rediscovering the Old Testament in a way that Judaism has not known for two thousand years. Moreover, Reform Jewish scholars are now studying the *New* Testament critically and sympathetically, a new phenomenon indeed in Jewish history. This, too, has opened the way to a new evaluation of the whole Bible, and to a new comprehension of what the Christian discovers in both Testaments.

The *Christian,* too, has wandered far from the Biblical God whom he shares with all three sections of Jewry, as is manifest in the terrible social abuses of this country, and in the appalling Biblical illiteracy of this generation. Thus both Jews and Christians, to the degree that they have missed the way, have failed to discover what both Testaments call 'life.' As both groups seek to understand what this word means, they can recall that they are already united by a reality which both are in the position to acknowledge. The Jew, on the one hand, believes that the Kingdom of God has not yet come, but that it will come in God's good time.

The Christian, on the other hand, believes that the Kingdom has begun to come in Christ, but is not yet fully here. This means that both Jews and Christians share a forward look to the final end of all God's ways and plans. Consequently, both may pray that when "Thy Kingdom comes," they may be found waiting, with their lamps lighted, and eagerly expecting the Bridegroom, as Hosea of old called our common Redeemer and our blessed God.

IX. The Jew's Place in God's Economy

Yet Jews cannot urge Christians, or Christians Jews, toward this *plērōma* by argument alone. It is when men and women confront each other as total persons, and not merely as minds, that a drawing together becomes possible. The Biblical word "to know" means much more than to have an intellectual grasp of a subject. It is used primarily of personal relations, between God and man, and between man and man. To "know" a man is not just to recognize that he is Mr. So-and-so. It is to *enter into his frame of reference* with loving understanding, and so to make contact with him as a thinking, sentient, believing being at the very point where he now is in his growth and development as a responsible child of God, *as* a Jew, or *as* a Christian, as the case may be, and not as a fellow member of the P.T.A. The Christian believes that the Holy Spirit is eager to aid God's children reach this true "knowledge" of each other; so the Christian is culpable if he does not pray for the Spirit's presence and interpreting power.

As we Christians come thus to "know" our friend, the Jew, we become aware of the irreplaceable value the Jew has even as he is, within the Christendom of the West. For the Jew is the "eternal protestant," as Israel Zangwill once called him, always *there,* right in our midst, confronting our social and religious life with a whole series of questions. Just by being *there,* he is asking us: "Are you Christians real Christians? Do you honestly suppose you are living up to your own knowledge of God in Christ? Am I, your Jewish neighbor, not the test case for your brotherly love that God himself has devised? Is there not something far from wholesome about your understanding of the Christian faith if in our time Western Christendom (not Eastern 'otherworldliness') has permitted the extermination of six millions of my people in the gas chambers?"

It is the will of God, then, that the Jewish people continues to *be*. So then, they are here! And *here* in almost every urban community and city suburb in North America. Which means, of course, as Paul puts it, that God has a purpose for his people still. Even although, in apostolic times, they did not "accept Christ," God did not therefore "cast off his people" (Rom. 11:1). The idea is unthinkable. We should constantly humble ourselves to remember that the ways of God are greater than our poor human understanding of them. Is it not a fact that all down through history God has taken the ways of men who did not necessarily believe in him or who even rebelled against him, and has woven their actions and their influence on the world into his majestic plan? The Bible itself shows him doing so in the case of men such as pagan king Nebuchadnezzar, or King Cyrus, the Zoroastrian by faith, or the agnostic Pontius Pilate, or the high priest Caiaphas, that loyal but obtuse Jew, and so on; and from seeing how God handled such men in that area of history which we call *Heilsgeschichte,* the story of God's saving purpose as recorded in the Bible, we receive a clue to understanding how God has overruled to his glory the freely executed influence of others such as Napoleon, Hitler, Stalin, and the rest. How infinitely more, then, has God used, and will continue to use, the influence of that *believing,* chosen instrument of his, the People of Israel? Let us therefore allow God to use the Jewish people to his glory, in their special relationship to us who are the Christian church. Let us permit the Jewish people to be what God has ordained that they should be, viz., his divinely ordained rebuke to the un-Christlikeness of Christendom, and the silent reproach of

God himself against the unlovingness of each one of us as Christians in this world.

Of course, however, nobody enjoys the rebuke of his conscience. So it is possible that a form of "religious anti-Semitism" may grow all unobserved in our hearts, since it is difficult for us to realize how much the Jew is the walking conscience of Christendom. But this antipathy to the Jew for being what God called him to be we must resolutely recognize for what it is, and refuse it the opportunity to take root in our minds.

X. Beyond Dialogue

Perhaps it is this secret of the Jew's continued existence in the world that God means us to appropriate now. It is true that the Jewish people neither "see nor understand" the significance of Christ as the New Testament speaks of him (Rom. 11:8), and that it is God's doing that this is so. But God has done this to them, Paul maintains, in order that their protest may lead *us* to accept Christ to an extent that Christendom as such does not do, nor ever yet has done. How, then, can we expect Jews to abandon their divinely given task of protest, and enter into our imperfect understanding of Christ? Yet (and here we are torn in two directions; and the Jew knows it, and pities us as he watches us), we *must* proclaim the gospel to him as to all men, simply because Christ is greater than our poor understanding and representation of him; for woe unto us if we preach not the gospel (I Cor. 9:16). But it must be the gospel of the *fullness* of Christ, of Christ as the arm of the Lord (Isa. 53:1), and not some emasculated denominational, far less "nondenominational" form of it; that is to say, it must be a gospel that has relevance for everything that the Jew is concerned about —not only the deepening of the inner, devotional life that is our common concern as Christians and Jews, but also the economics of the nations, the feeding of the hungry, the furtherance of true race relations, even the scientific quest for the stars. And the Jew must proclaim to us that the *Torah* is indeed concerned with great areas of life that an emasculated Christianity ignores. That is why the Jew has so much to contribute to the *plērōma,* or fullness, to supplement the faith of that kind of Christian who, forgetting the faith of the New Testament, that Christ is Lord of all, preaches only the personal salvation of individual souls.

If it is the case, however, as Jews believe, that the Old Testament contains God's full and final revelation, and, as Jesus believed, that *everything* concerning himself is to be found in the pages of the Old Testament alone (Luke 24:27), then it is obvious that the one thing above all others that we have to do together as Jews and Christians, now in these days of new mutual understanding and respect, is to study anew with each other's help this Old Testament that we possess in common.

BIBLIOGRAPHY

The authors of the chapters in this book have selected, each for his own contribution, brief lists of books for suggested further reading. They are as follows:

Chapter One

Glazer, Nathan, *American Judaism.* The University of Chicago Press, 1957.

Gordon, Albert I., *Jews in Transition.* The University of Minnesota Press, 1949; and *Jews in Suburbia.* Beacon Press, Inc., 1959.

Hartstein, Jacob I., ed., *The Jews in American History.* B'nai B'rith, 1701 K Street, N.W., Washington, D.C.

Sklare, Marshall, *Conservative Judaism.* The Free Press of Glencoe, Inc., 1955.

Weisberg, Harold, *American Judaism: The Next Century* and *Perspectives on Jewish Religion.* B'nai B'rith.

Chapter Two

Blauw, Johannes, *The Missionary Nature of the Church.* McGraw-Hill Book Company, Inc., 1962.

Jocz, Jakob, *A Theology of Election.* S.P.C.K., London, 1958.

Knight, George A. F., *Law and Grace.* The Westminster Press, 1962.

Rowley, H. H., *The Biblical Doctrine of Election.* London: Lutterworth Press, 3d ed., 1953.

Chapter Three

Heschel, Abraham J., *The Prophets.* Harper & Row, Publishers, Inc., 1963.

Knight, H., *The Hebrew Prophetic Consciousness.* London: Lutterworth Press, 1947.

Lindblom, J., *Prophecy in Ancient Israel.* Muhlenberg Press, 1962.

Chapter Four

Johnson, Aubrey R., *Sacral Kingship in Ancient Israel.* Cardiff: University of Wales Press, 1955.

Klausner, Joseph, *The Messianic Idea in Israel: From Its Beginning to the Completion of the Mishnah,* tr. from the 3d Hebrew ed. by W. F. Stinespring. The Macmillan Company, 1955.

Mowinckel, Sigmund, *He That Cometh.* Abingdon Press, 1956.

Silver, Abba Hillel, *A History of Messianic Speculation in Israel: From the First Through the Seventeenth Centuries.* Beacon Press, Inc., with new preface, 1959.

Chapter Six

Piper, Otto; Jocz, Jakob; and Floreen, Harold, *The Church Meets Judaism.* Augsburg Publishing House, 1960.

Chapter Seven

Buber, Martin, *Two Types of Faith.* The Macmillan Company, 1952.

Davies, W. D., *Paul and Rabbinic Judaism.* The Macmillan Company, 1955.

Gillet, Lev, *Communion in the Messiah.* Lutterworth Press, London, 1942.

Grant, F. C., *Ancient Judaism and the New Testament.* The Macmillan Company, 1959.

Heschel, Abraham J., *God in Search of Man.* The Jewish Publication Society of America, Meridian Books, 1959.

Heschel, Abraham J., *The Prophets.*

Knight, George A. F., *A Christian Theology of the Old Testament.* Board of Christian Education, The Presbyterian Church in the U.S., 1959.

Knight, George A. F., *From Moses to Paul: A Christological Study in the Light of Our Hebraic Heritage.* London: Lutterworth Press, 1949.

Kaufmann, Yehezkel, *The Religion of Israel.* The University of Chicago Press, 1960.

Moore, George Foot, *Judaism in the First Centuries of the Christian Era: The Age of the Tannaim*, 3 vols. Harvard University Press, 1927–1930.

Rankin, Oliver Shaw, *Jewish Religious Polemic*. Edinburgh: Edinburgh University Press, 1956.

Williams, Arthur Lukyn, *Talmudic Judaism and Christianity*. The Macmillan Company, 1933, paper.

Chapter Eight

Hebert, A. G., *The Old Testament from Within*. Oxford University Press, 1962.

Herberg, Will, *Protestant—Catholic—Jew: An Essay in American Religious Sociology*. Doubleday & Company, Inc., 1955.

Olson, Bernhard E., *Faith and Prejudice*. Yale University Press, 1963.

Chapter Nine

Eckardt, A. Roy, *The Elder and the Younger Brother: Dimensions of the Jewish-Christian Encounter*. Holt, Rinehart and Winston, Inc., 1965.

Hochhuth, Rolf, *The Representative* (*Der Stellvertreter*). London: Methuen & Co., Ltd., 1963.

Isaac, Jules, *Has Anti-Semitism Roots in Christianity?* tr. by Dorothy and James Parkes. National Conference of Christians and Jews, 1961.

Tumin, Melvin M., *An Inventory and Appraisal of Research on American Anti-Semitism*. Freedom Books, 1961.

Chapter Ten

Hedenquist, Göte, ed., *The Church and the Jewish People*. Edinburgh House Press, London, 1954.

Jocz, Jakob, *The Jewish People and Jesus Christ: A Study in the Relationship Between the Jewish People and Jesus Christ*. London: S.P.C.K., 1949.

Menkus, Belden, ed., *Meet the American Jew*. Broadman Press, 1963.

Noveck, Simon, *Contemporary Jewish Thought—a Reader*. B'nai B'rith Department of Adult Jewish Education, Clinton, Mass., 1963.

Oesterreicher, John M., ed., *The Bridge: A Yearbook of Judaeo-Christian Studies,* Vols. I to IV. Pantheon Books, 1955–1962. (A Roman Catholic series).

Parkes, James, *A History of the Jewish People.* Quadrangle Books, Inc., 1963.

Schoeps, Hans Joachim, *The Jewish-Christian Argument: A History of Theologies in Conflict.* Holt, Rinehart and Winston, Inc., 1963.

Von Balthasar, Hans Urs, *Martin Buber and Christianity: A Dialogue Between Israel and the Church.* English translation, The Macmillan Company, 1962 (Roman Catholic).

Yates, George A., ed. *In Spirit and in Truth: A Jewish-Christian Symposium.* London: Hodder & Stoughton, Ltd., 1934.

GLOSSARY

'am: Hebrew word for "people," but normally reserved for Israel as the people of God. Translated in the New Testament by the Greek *laos.*

Anti-Semitism: Hatred and denigration of the Jewish people. (That the specific term "anti-Semitism" was not invented until the nineteenth century is thus of no consequence in the present context.)

Apocalyptic: A body of literature, mainly non-Biblical, similar in some respects to the prophetic writings, but preoccupied by the ultimate goals of history, and characterized by visions, complex symbolism, and usually by pseudonymity. Biblical examples: Daniel in the Old Testament, II Esdras in the Apocrypha, The Revelation to John in the New Testament.

Archetype: An original image or pattern from which various representations are derived.

'Asham: Guilt offering, as in Lev. ch. 5, etc.

Bar Mitzvah: "Son of the law"; religious maturity of a Jewish boy on reaching the age of 13 years and one day; equivalent to Christian confirmation.

Christian theology: The rational derivation of spiritual and ethical judgment from the presuppositions of faith, primarily the Christian faith.

Collective unconscious: The deposit of historical and ancestral experience within the social self of man in ways of which he is ordinarily unaware.

Enoch: A composite intertestamental work of great importance, not to be found in the Apocrypha.

Gemara: Another name for Talmud as distinct from Mishnah.

Gen. R.: A Rabbinical commentary on Genesis, from about the sixth century A.D. Similarly, Lev. R. or Num. R.

Goy: Hebrew for "nation" other than Israel, translated in the New Testament by *ethnos*.

Ḥesed: A Hebrew noun that describes the content of the covenant relationship in the Old Testament, with no one English equivalent. RSV translates as "steadfast love." But it is also rendered as "mercy," "loving-kindness," etc.

Midrash (pl., midrashim): Homiletical exposition of Scripture as handed down by tradition.

Mishnah: Oldest collection of Rabbinic legislative code.

Mitzvah (pl., mitzvoth): Commandment, precept, meritorious deed.

Nephesh: A Hebrew word for which we have no equivalent. It must not be identified with the Platonic "soul" as distinct from the body, for it includes what we call both soul and body, along with all the physical appetites. It is the whole person, not just as an individual, but also in his relationship to society.

Pentateuch: The books of the law, or Torah; the first five books of the Old Testament.

Pesikta: A commentary on the Biblical lessons for the Jewish feast days and the more important Sabbaths, compiled about A.D. 700.

Pirke Aboth, or Sayings of the Fathers: A tractate of the Mishnah. It may be read in English translation in the Authorized Jewish Prayer Book.

Plērōma: Literally "fullness," but used in the New Testament with the special meaning discussed in the text.

Praeparatio evangelica: (Latin), preparation of the gospel; used in the wider sense of the whole action of God in preparing men's hearts and minds for the gospel, in the narrower sense for the Old Testament revelation as preparing Israel for the coming of the Messiah.

Prōton: Literally "first"; but used in the New Testament with a new content and meaning.

Rashi: Lived in France from 1040 to 1105. **Sa'adyah Gaon** flourished in the next century, and **David Qimḥi's** dates are 1160–1235. The others mentioned in the text follow these three scholars in the next century.

Shalom: While often translated "peace," means much more than a mere cessation of hostilities. It represents the full, complete, healthy, whole, integrated life that God has in mind for his people.

Shekinah: A technical term used by the rabbis to represent the special presence of God. Buxtorf's dictionary defines it as: "Habitation, divinity, glory, the divine majesty dwelling among men."

Talmud: Commentary on the Mishnah dating from the period of third to sixth century A.D.

Targum Cant.: The Aramaic Targum or translation in Aramaic, with much exposition, of The Song of Songs.

Targum Onkelos: Translation of the Pentateuch into Aramaic. Written down only in the early Christian centuries, yet probably enshrining the oral translation of the Hebrew used in synagogues before Christ.

Testimonia: (Latin) "testimonies"; texts from the Old Testament assembled by the early Christians as bearing witness to the person and work of Jesus as the Messiah.

Theodicy: An understanding of "the rule of God," particularly in relation to his allowing evil to exist.

Tobit: A quasi-historical book written with a moral purpose, to be found in the intertestamental literature.

Torah: Pentateuch; in a wider sense Rabbinic instruction in the life and teaching of Judaism.

Tractates: In the Babylonian Talmud these are identified as "T. B. San.," etc., i.e., Talmud Babli Sanhedrin, etc.

Tsedaqah: Usually translated "righteousness." But Second Isaiah defines it by making it parallel with "salvation." It speaks of compassionate love, which in its turn creates a changed relationship toward God in other people.